CONTENTS

Acknowledgements

Prologue: Divine Wedding

ACKNOWLEDGEMENTS

I would like to dedicate this book to my family, friends and acquaintances that were instrumental in our quest for hope.

Cassidy Moore, thank you for teaching me so much about determination and never giving up. You are courageous and an inspiration to so many who are blessed to know you.

Channing Moore, you are the best big sister anyone could hope for. Thank you for encouraging your sister and setting a good example for her.

Chad Moore, my husband, who blessed me with these two beautiful girls. Thank you for accepting and loving me, and the girls through all the tough times.

To my parents, Gary and Dianne Tarpley, who have supported and believed in me. Thank you for your unconditional love and giving of your time and resources to your children and grandchildren.

To my sister, Alicia Fife, who has always been my best friend and her family Dale, Dylan, Summer and Jadyn. I have so many memories of the kids growing up together. Each of you has been there for us throughout our journey with Cassidy, especially Jadyn who has looked up to her and loved her so much.

Thanks to all of our friends that helped us through the hard times with your emotional support. Lauri Vardeman, thanks for insisting that I get on Medicaid. Vickie and Mic Parvin, introduced us to Margaret whose father got Cassidy accepted to Scottish Rite Hospital for Children. Tracy and Matthew Rast shared resources, and information for cerebral palsy.

We owe Pastor Randy Frazee special thanks for his gifts in teaching God's word, and for sharing the story about his son. You touched our whole family and brought us closer to God.

To all the nurses and doctors who treated Cassidy and me at Harris Methodist Hospital, Cooks Children's Hospital, Arlington Memorial Hospital, and Scottish Rite Hospital.

To all the schools and programs, ECI, and Arlington ISD, that has been there for Cassidy. Each of her teachers has influenced her for a lifetime.

To my Aunt and Uncle, Virginia and Dale Presnell who volunteered to take Cassidy for treatment in New Mexico, and have shared her story with many others who have also had great results.

To Jessica Walton, who married my cousin Cole Presnell, and prepared the dinner seating arrangements at her wedding. You placed us next to your uncle, Kevin Hennelly, who introduced us all to Dr. Hao. We are blessed to have you in the family.

A special thanks to Dr. Jason Hao who has mastered the technique of Chinese scalp acupuncture that helps so many people. You have given our family hope for full recovery. Cassidy's life has been transformed. We will never be able to thank you enough for the happiness you have given our precious daughter, Cassidy.

Most of all, I thank my Lord and Savior for never leaving or forsaking me when I have, at times, left you. Thank you for guiding me through all circumstances in life that led to this transformation in Cassidy. It is my prayer that you will use us to transform others, and give people with neurological disabilities hope and healing.

(PROLOGUE)

DIVINE WEDDING

Chad, Cassidy, and I left Arlington, Texas mid-day on February 25, 2012. We were going to my cousin, Cole's, wedding in Austin. We arrived in Austin with just enough time to get checked into the hotel and get changed for the ceremony that evening.

Cassidy, 12, is our youngest daughter. She really wanted to look especially pretty for this special occasion. Cassidy had a stroke in utero that had partially paralyzed her whole right side, so I helped her to put on make-up and curl her long, light brown hair. She was transformed into a much older looking young lady. Although she is very pretty, she had always felt self-conscious, especially in groups of strangers. We rushed to the lobby of the hotel to join my parents and my sister and her family. We were a little sad that my sister's oldest two and our oldest daughter couldn't attend because they were in college.

The wedding venue was a large, beautiful historic home in the center of Austin. We arrived at dusk on a cool winter afternoon to see peacocks wandering the grounds, and the lovely area that had been set up under the trees for their wedding. Everything was sweet and lovely.

After the ceremony, everyone was invited inside to the dining room for champagne, dinner, and dancing. I followed my family to the area where they were sitting only to find that Chad, Cassidy and I weren't sitting with any of them. Instead, we were seated across the dance floor at a table with some of the bride's relatives. We didn't know anyone at our table. I leaned over and whispered to my husband, "We must be the black sheep of the family." He nodded his head in agreement and my daughter gave me a disappointed look. She knew she would be very uncomfortable meeting new people and have them want to shake her hand. Shaking hands always caused her embarrassment, because her right hand was always in a fist.

Once everyone was seated, the waiters were quick to fill glasses and pass the appetizers. We all introduced ourselves to each other. We learned that we were seated with the bride's uncles from

New Mexico. The waiter's brought our entrees of steak and lobster. I instinctively grabbed Cassidy's plate, cut up her meat, and placed it back in front of her. I looked up to see people staring at me. I realized how strange this must look, because she was clearly old enough to handle this task on her own. Kevin, the uncle sitting next to me, asked me why I did that for her. I explained that she had a stroke that affected the right side of her body. I went on to explain that she had been diagnosed with cerebral palsy, hemiplegia (partial paralysis), and lacked peripheral vision in her right eye. Kevin informed me that he knew a doctor in Santa Fe, New Mexico that specialized in helping stroke victims and people with disorders of the central nervous system. I told Kevin that we had taken her to the finest doctors and hospitals; however, each one of them told us that there was nothing that could reverse the effects of a stroke. Kevin asked for my email address and offered to send me more information about the doctor. "Sure", I replied, but that was more like a "sure....whatever".

I didn't expect to ever hear from him again, thinking he would forget about us. I had not been offered hope before and no longer expected it.

Months later, I realized that I would never refer to Kevin as a stranger, but instead as our angel.

We didn't know that sitting at that table to dine next to Kevin that particular evening would forever change our lives. Kevin had been through a difficult emotional time just prior to the wedding, and he and his brother almost didn't attend the wedding because of their own family tragedies. Thank goodness they were there, as this turned out to be a life changing experience for our family.

We are telling everyone with similar physical issues about the doctor in New Mexico, so they, or their family member can be helped and healed. We know we were divinely guided to sit next to Kevin that night. Jesus, the good shepherd, loves and looks after all his sheep. It also taught me a lesson. God is involved in all aspects of our lives.

THE BC YEARS

(YEARS BEFORE CASSIDY)

When Chad and I decided to get married, we discussed our plans for the future. Chad had a lucrative job with a food manufacturing company, and we were both taking classes at a local community college. Getting a college degree was very important, so we agreed to wait until I graduated to start a family.

Several years later, when I was only a few months away from having my degree, I stopped taking birth control. I knew that it could take some time to get pregnant. Because I could now see the light at the end of the tunnel, I felt we were being very realistic and practical in our planning. When I chose to discontinue birth control, I remember praying that if I was meant to be a mom and a really good mom, to please bless me with a child. If I would not be a good mom, I prayed to not allow me to get pregnant.

Graduation day finally arrived. It was time to celebrate. This was a big deal. I felt that my parents had given up on me actually getting my degree. I always struggled through school because I couldn't sit still long enough to read a book or finish my homework. I always wanted to sing, dance, run, and play. I promised myself that I could do this and really wanted it.

To celebrate my graduation, my sister, brother in law, Chad and I planned a camping trip to New Braunfels, Texas, so we could float the river. It is a beautiful river, and always has crowds of young people anxious to enjoy the water, and fun. We decided to go together in one vehicle. They came to our house to pick us up. As we were busy loading the car, my sister gave me a couple of pregnancy tests that had expired dates on them.

They already had 2 children and had no plans of having any more. I thought she was silly for giving these to me because I didn't intend to have kids right away. I just graduated and wanted time to celebrate.

While we were on the trip, I began to feel funny. I felt bloated and everything started to taste different than usual. That happens to most women on a monthly basis so I partied through it.

 The week after our trip, I was at home doing some house cleaning when I got dizzy. I thought that was strange. I wonder? It has only been a month since I graduated, and here I am taking another test. This time I actually wanted to fail the test. Oh no, I passed. It was positive. Then I remembered the test had expired. I made a doctor's appointment to make sure. The doctor confirmed that my celebration must come to an end. On my way home, I found myself telling God that I didn't mean that I wanted kids right away. But I gladly and proudly accepted this blessing in our lives.

The pregnancy was fine until the fifth month when my husband woke me at 5 a.m. He had panic in his voice. He told me I was bleeding a lot. I immediately called the doctor. The doctor said not to worry and to call back if it happened again. I hung up confused as how this was something to not worry about.
I continued to bleed and ended up staying the night at the hospital. I was released the next day. The doctor said he wasn't sure why I was bleeding. It

was possible that it was placenta previa and to call if it happened again.

The rest of the pregnancy went well until delivery day. The due date was February 5th, but on February 10th, I was on my way to my doctor's appointment. While sitting in the waiting room, my water broke. They quickly took me to a delivery room. After several hours, an anesthesiologist appeared and my pain quickly disappeared. But my need to push also disappeared. After several more hours of pushing, I hear the doctor announce, "We have meconium here."

My room quickly filled with nurses. The baby had a bowel movement while still in utero, which could be deadly if the meconium filled her lungs. When my daughter, Channing, was delivered, the nurses quickly took her. They began shoving tubes up her nose to get all the meconium out of her. She was a healthy 8 pounds 3 ounces; however, she and I were both running a fever. I was finally able to hold my sweet baby girl after twenty-four hours when our fevers subsided.

HARD AT WORK

Chad came home from work and I greeted him. "Hi, honey. How was your day?" I expected the usual response, "fine". But on that day he said, "Not so good." When I asked what was wrong, he informed me that his company announced that they were shutting the food manufacturing plant down. My heart sank and landed in a tight knot in my stomach. My mind was racing. What would we do? He told me this would be a six month process. Thankfully, all management would receive a severance check, which would get us through until he could find another job, when Channing was older. I didn't want to have to leave her to get a job just yet.

Chad looked for a job to transition into when the plant closed. The only opportunities that came his way were all out of state. I told him that I loved him and would go with him anywhere, but with a new baby, I really did not want to move cross country. I had no desire to leave our doctors, friends, and family, especially since my family only lived about ten minutes away. I felt overwhelmed, worried and panicked. What were we going to do? As always, especially at a time of crisis, I prayed. I tried to pray all the time, but knew that I prayed more in times of crisis and need.

Chad had been working since high school. He had started at the bottom and risen to management. He knew a lot about managing employees, food safety, and hard work. My degree was in sales and marketing. There had to be opportunities for us in the metropolitan area where we lived. We couldn't find anything that fit, and we were getting desperate. We networked and talked to as many people as possible to get ideas, and to find what was available.

Then I had the bright idea that we should start our own business. I walked into the bedroom where Chad sat at the desk working on the computer. I announced to him with great enthusiasm my brilliant idea. He replied, "That is ridiculous." I told him that we had friends that had their own businesses. My grandfather started his own successful business. I told him that I thought if they could, then we could. I told him that I thought with his severance money and our 401K we should be able to get something started.

One Sunday morning, while reading the paper, I was drawn to an article in the business section. I read, "For sale 3 sandwich franchises, contact……" I thought, "This is it!" We knew a man who owned several Subway stores. He had talked about them frequently, and seemed to be doing well. I worked on convincing Chad and my parents that this was a great idea. We found ourselves writing a business plan, putting together profit and loss statements, and attending many meetings with the bank. We also worked on franchise fees, training, and said a lot of prayers. I asked God that if this was meant to be and if this was the business for us, then please let this happen.

By July, 1995, we were the proud owner of three Subway sandwich franchises. On the third day of ownership, God answered my prayers, and the answer was "NO!" We were so new to this that we were still trying to get a handle on running 3 stores. It was a big task. We received a call from the police near closing time. They said that a sixteen year old employee had been taken to the hospital with a bad injury. He had seriously cut himself while opening a can of olives.

Chad and I rushed to the store to find blood everywhere. We stayed at the store for hours cleaning and sanitizing everything so we could open the next morning. Thankfully, our insurance covered the ambulance, medical, therapy, and all prescriptions for our employee.

 The parents even met with us and thanked us for the support and made a comment that "things happen for a reason". They said they felt that this accident saved him from a more serious injury from football. Then when their son turned eighteen, we received legal papers notifying us that we were being sued for negligence. We didn't feel there was any negligence, because there were signs posted in every store on safety rules concerning this very incident. We went into mediation, where they asked for several hundred thousand dollars. They ended up settling for $6,000. Of course, this felt like a huge amount considering we were up to our necks in debt on the stores.

That was only one of many headaches that we incurred. Our stores had several break-ins, employee theft, employee attendance issues, and vandalism. At least once, we found employees using our meat scale to weigh their drugs. We chalked it all up to the cost of doing business.

Regardless of how the employees treated us, we wanted to treat our employees well. While we owned the stores, unemployment was very low. We needed good employees that were vested in long term employment. Turnover was killing us, so we thought if we offered a benefits package maybe we could attract an older and more mature employee. We needed insurance for our employees and ourselves as well, so we began getting quotes from several different health insurance carriers. The costs were unbelievable.

Chad and I wanted insurance for ourselves. We really wanted another child before I turned thirty, and our Cobra insurance had long since expired. I began to get angry at all the insurance companies. They all required you to provide maternity coverage for group policies, but would not cover pregnancy coverage until the policy had been in effect for 1 year. I couldn't believe they were serious. Most of our employees were teenagers, and didn't even stay with us for a year. When we talked to our employees and asked who would opt in for the insurance, not one of them wanted it. Since it takes at least 3 people to be considered a group policy, we had to table the idea for a while. Each year we would revisit getting insurance and the same problems continued to recur. I stayed angry and frustrated.

One evening in January 1999, Chad and I had a long serious talk about our future. We discussed insurance options again. We both agreed that we just couldn't afford it. We decided that Channing would be an only child. It wasn't just because of insurance. How could we run the stores and take care of a newborn? We were spending the majority of time working. We argued over which one of us would get "fixed". He was adamant that it shouldn't be him. I argued that I would have to miss weeks of work to recover. Who would take care of Channing, and help him run the stores? It would also cost more for me to have my tubes tied because it is surgery that requires a hospital. We agreed that I would discuss this issue with the doctor when I had my annual checkup.

Two weeks later I went to the gynecologist. The nurse called me back while handing me a cup for a urine sample. After the usual wait, she knocked on the door. She entered with a big grin on her face, "Congratulations, you're pregnant." I burst into tears. The nurse's enthusiasm quickly turned into concern. She put her arm around me and tried to console me by saying, "This is a good thing."

I continued to sob, shaking my head, saying, "I can't, I can't." When I could get control and quit crying, I explained our situation of a heavy workload and no insurance. In fact, I had planned to talk to the doctor today about sterilization. She again reassured me that everything would be okay. The doctor would negotiate with us on a reduced fee with the payments spread out over the pregnancy. I went home with a handful of brochures and filled with anxiety.

On my drive home, I continued to cry. As I wiped my tears, I talked to God. I was angry. "God, you know our finances. You know I can't have a baby when I need to help run the stores. Channing deserves my attention. How can I do this?" I pleaded. Then I realized that I had been pregnant when Chad and I made our decision not to have any more children. God had to be laughing at us when we made that decision. My thoughts and tears soon turned to how I was going to break the news to my parents. They already helped us so much when we weren't able to make the bills, and that was often. I knew that we couldn't afford any additional expenses and I didn't want to burden their finances even more.

As I pulled into the driveway, I dreaded telling Chad. I anticipated that he would have the same reaction as I did. I became sick to my stomach walking through the door. When he saw me he asked, "What is wrong?"

 My eyes were red and puffy with mascara running down my face. I started sobbing again. I finally composed myself enough to tell him that we were expecting a baby. He wiped my face and said, "That is great news. Why are you crying?"

What planet did he come from", I thought to myself. I looked at him perplexed, "I can't do this".

"We will find a way", he replied with great confidence.

We had been working long hours to keep everything running smoothly, which became impossible. The town in which two of our stores were located was making a large road improvement that directly affected one of our stores. It was difficult to get to because of detours, so our sales plummeted. We had a huge payment to the bank every month on our business loan and it didn't matter that our sales were down by a third. Profitability was going out the window. We were just praying to keep the stores going until the road project was over. My parents had co-signed our business note. If we couldn't make these stores profitable, Chad and I, and my parents would all be wiped out financially. I was already putting Channing into an inexpensive mother's day out program at a local church and my mother helped with her care. I had to because we couldn't afford childcare. There was no way we could cut expenses. We were barely able to stay afloat.

Over the next few months, I would switch back and forth from times of acceptance to panic. I had no idea how we would pull this off. It seemed every question led to another question. My mind was reeling. I thought that I had a lot of faith, but our problems seemed too many and too big. I just prayed for God to help us through another day.

GOD, ARE YOU KIDDING ME?

I was now six weeks into my pregnancy. My sister, Alicia, called to invite us over for a cook-out. Several of their friends and neighbors would be there. I responded with my normal, "Sounds good, but it depends on the stores". All of our employees actually showed up for their shifts, so we were able to attend. We really needed a night out. It was fun for us to be around other people just relaxing and having a few laughs. It seemed our lives were totally wrapped up in employees and customers.

That night at the cook-out, I had a conversation with Laurie, a good friend and neighbor of my sister. I had known Lauri for about 14 years at that time and she had worked as a social worker for many years. She started the conversation with, "I hear congratulations are in order".

I gave her a shrug and a meek, "Thank you". I was very honest with her about our whole situation.

She brought up the chance of getting Medicaid. In a firm and insistent voice, she said, "Allison, you have worked since the day I first met you. You have paid taxes into the system for this very reason. That is why Medicaid exists. It is for people just like you that are hardworking people that fall on hard times and can't afford health care."

I shook my head in disagreement, although in my head, everything she said made sense. I felt that I would humiliate my family if I followed her advice. The more I thought about it, the more it seemed that she was right. I knew my parents would give us money to pay for the baby, but I did not want to be more of a burden on them financially. I decided that I would at least apply and see what happened.

I arrived at the local Social Services office to fill out my application and turn in several years of income tax returns. I felt like a fish out of water. I was very uncomfortable, and one of the few there without an entourage of children or a mate. One man was throwing up in the trash can. Another man was going through another trash can looking for who knows what. I felt humbled and humiliated as I quietly waited my turn, while people seemed to stare at me. I know these people probably felt just like I did. The process strips you of any dignity you may possess.

After a lengthy wait, I finally heard my name called. The clerk immediately informed me that I was over qualified.

"How can that be?" I asked.

"You put that you have three vehicles on your application. Good-bye," she said, as she passed the application back to me.

"Excuse me," I replied," the Maxima was bought before we were married and it is paid off. The truck was purchased at auction for $750, and the minivan was leased."

Abruptly she responded, "Sorry, those are the rules. Who is next?"

"Wait! Do you have a supervisor?" I said as calmly as I could.

"Yes", she answered.

"I would like to speak with them, please," I tried to sound professional.

She told me to have a seat and she would call me when the supervisor was available. An hour later, I heard my name and was led down the hallway to an office. The supervisor heard my plea.

I was told, "I'm sorry, but these are the rules and there is nothing that I can do." I had spent half my day in an office where I clearly did not feel that I belonged. Darn it! I wasn't going to give in that easy. My friend, Lauri's words kept ringing in my head. The system was meant and built for tax paying citizens like me. I wasn't going down without a fight.

By the end of the day, I made my way to the top decision maker. I gave him my application, tax returns, and stated my case. He replied, "My wife is self- employed, and I understand." He then gave me the approval. It was an exhausting and stressful day, but I was so thrilled to have fought for what I thought was fair and right. A huge weight was lifting off my shoulders.

When I went to the doctor for my first official visit at three months, I was told that everything was good and appeared normal. I continued to work at the Subway stores with Channing, now four years old, in tow. During lunch rushes I would often sit her on the counter while I ran the cash register. She would take the customers money and hand it to me. Then she would hand the change to the customer. Petite little Channing was the only one to ever receive tips. When she was tired or bored, I would take her to the back office. I would pop a Barney tape into the security VCR. We would often hear her singing and clapping. She was born an old soul, and seemed to understand things going on in our lives that we never told her. Thank goodness she was such a good, sweet child.

TV ON THE MOVE

My older sister, Alicia, was a flight attendant. She could work for three or four days in a row, but then have three or four days off. She had always been a professional worrier. She worried more than anyone I knew, even more than my parents. On her day off, she would call me every morning as soon as she took her two kids to school. On this particular morning, I had been working from home paying bills, completing reports, and scheduling employees for the week ahead. When she called, I was ready for a break. I took the phone into the den and sat down facing the TV. At some point during the conversation, I said, "Whoa!"

She asked what was wrong.

"That was so weird! The TV just moved", I replied.

She agreed that it was strange, and started asking me a series of questions, "Did it really move?

Did you bump into it? Did you just have a feeling that it moved?"

I told her that I didn't know, but it was very strange. She told me to call the doctor. I didn't feel that was necessary because I had my normal checkup coming the following week.

She insisted that I hang up and call the doctor's office, and to then call her back. I did it just to appease her. I felt they would probably tell me that I was losing my mind or I was a hypochondriac.

When I called the doctor's office, I explained that I had just seen my TV move. The receptionist replied with a question, "Did you just say that you saw your TV move? Okay, let me get the nurse, please hold."

I could only imagine the conversation on the other end of the line. I expected the receptionist to recommend a mental hospital. That actually would have sounded okay with me. I needed a getaway. Much to my surprise the nurse came on the line and said, "Mrs. Moore? How soon can you get here?"

I said, "I'm sure it was just nothing. My sister insisted that I call."

The nurse replied, "I am sure you are right, but we would like to check you out." When I hung up, I quickly called Alicia. I told her that I would check back with her after I saw the doctor.

When I arrived at the doctor's office, they took me back immediately, which had never happened. The nurse weighed me in, took my blood pressure, and then left the exam room. The doctor came in shortly thereafter, sat down and said, "Well, your blood pressure is high. That could be a sign of the onset of toxemia."

My doctor asked several questions about diet and stress. I laughed and told him, "I paid bills earlier this morning. Maybe that is what caused my blood pressure to go up."

He said, "Yes, that would do it. I'll be able tell more when you come back next week for your scheduled visit."

My following appointment went much better, although my blood pressure was a little high. It was much better than the previous week. The doctor told me that since I made so much progress that he would like to see me again in two weeks. If that one turned out good, then he would put me back on monthly visits.

When the doctor first mentioned toxemia, also known as preeclampsia, I went home and looked it up in my book <u>What To Expect When You're Expecting.</u> There were a lot of symptoms listed, headache, dizziness, vomiting/nausea, high blood pressure and water retention. Other than the time when the TV moved, I had no more dizzy spells. My only other symptom was elevated blood pressure.

I was really excited about the next appointment. I had been feeling great, and it had been a month since the mention of toxemia. I was ready to scratch all symptoms off the list. At my appointment, the nurse performed the weight, urine, and blood pressure test. All the while, I was staring at her trying to see any positive or negative reaction. There was no reaction, but she left to get the doctor. When the doctor came in he informed me that my blood pressure went up substantially, and ordered me to bed rest. I was told to stay off my feet as much as possible until my next appointment in two weeks.

I had mixed emotions. My first thought was that I couldn't do bed rest. I had a four year old, and I had to help run three stores. The other thought was that I needed to get some rest. I stayed home and off my feet as much as possible. That was really difficult. Chad was working night and day. I thought if he would bring the deposits home, I could be of help to him. I would add them up and get them to the bank. That required only a walk to and from the car.

At that time, I was President of the Ambassador's for the Chamber of Commerce. They had strict attendance requirements so I attended those occasional events. Of course, I still had to take care of Channing's needs. I limited household chores, but laundry and dishes had to be done.

Needless to say, the next doctor's appointment came with a scolding. The doctor said, "When I say bed rest, I mean total bed rest. You must lie on your left side only. You may get up to go the bathroom and to shower once a week."

It would have been easier to meet his demands if I had felt badly, but I felt fine. Chad rearranged the furniture so I could watch television while on my left side. Each morning he would take Channing over to my mother's house across town, and pick her up on his way home. She often spent the night with my parents on days when the stores demanded that he be there late at night. He was working so hard to not only manage the stores without my help, but now he had to worry about taking care of me.

The next few months were miserable. I was in and out of the hospital. Each time they would keep me for two or three days. These trips were caused by my blood pressure reaching dangerous levels. The problem was that as long as I was on my left side everything was okay. If I sat up or stood up, it would soar to dangerous levels. Of course, on days when I had doctor's appointments it would skyrocket. The times when I had to be up getting ready, traveling, and sitting in the waiting room affected my blood pressure. The worse it was, the more often the doctor would want to see me. I began to swell. That didn't seem abnormal to me for a very pregnant woman. Chad disagreed and told me that my nose was now taking up a large amount of real estate on my face. He also informed me that my toes looked like sausages. I disagreed with him, and I still felt fine. I did admit that I couldn't wear most of my shoes. In my last trimester, it even became painful to write.

In August, about eleven weeks before my due date, I moved in with my parents. My mother demanded it because Chad had to work so much, and there was no one to help me. She also didn't trust that I was staying off my feet. She knew my personality leaned toward the hyperactive. Telling me to lie down all day and all night and not get up was like telling a fish not to swim. I would go to our home on week-ends. Our teenage employees could put in more hours on week-ends without interfering with their school. That allowed Chad a little more time away from the stores.

I was humiliated to have to live with Mom and Dad and be dependent on them again. Mother was a great caregiver, arranging everything to make my situation as comfortable as possible. She gave me a bell to ring if I needed anything at all and came to check on me while also watching over Channing. It was very stressful for everybody. Chad would come over when he left work, so he could spend time with us. Everybody was stressed over finances, taking care of business, and my health. There didn't seem to be enough hours in the day for them. Finances were a huge stress factor for my whole family and at this point, my health was declining.

Even with a television to watch and family coming and going from my room, it was extremely difficult to stay in one position day after day. I spent a lot of time just thinking. While lost in my battle between worry and faith, I wrote a poem about my unborn baby.

Birth of an Angel

Lord, bless and be with me as I raise this child,

With wings so delicate, meek and mild.

Please help me to take care of these precious wings,

When to spread, stroke, clip, or other special things.

I know one day this child's wings will be fully grown,

And I pray, dear Lord that they can fly alone.

On Friday, September 17th, I had a scheduled doctor's appointment. His office was across the street from the hospital. I laid down in my parents van on the way to his office to try and keep my blood pressure down. Of course, we had to wait to see the doctor. When they called me to the exam room, they did the usual urine, blood pressure, tests. When the doctor came into the exam room, he announced, "This is not good. I want you to check in the hospital and stay until you have the baby."

I cried. I still had six weeks until my due date. I couldn't stand being there for three days at a time. How could I endure six weeks?

The doctor said, "There was some blood in your urine. That could indicate that you are becoming eclampsic. This is when a woman is at risk of seizures, kidney and liver failure."

I protested having to go to the hospital right away. I begged him to let me go home for the weekend. That was the only time I got to spend at home with my husband and daughter. I promised him that I would return on Monday morning by six with everything packed and prepared to stay for six weeks or until the birth of our baby girl.

The doctor finally agreed and made me promise to check into the hospital by six on Monday morning. My mom and I gathered our things and made our way down the long hall to the elevators. While waiting for the elevator to arrive, we heard, "Mrs. Moore, Mrs. Moore, please wait!"

We looked around to see the doctor running down the hall. He approached us and said, "I don't feel good about this at all. I want you to get checked into the hospital right now. Go to the third floor maternity department and they will be expecting you."

I began wailing and crying. This couldn't be happening. Not only did I not want to check in for a six weeks stay, I was scared. As we entered the third floor maternity department, the nurses noticed my tears. They asked, "Are you that upset to see us again?" We were starting to get to know each other after so many stays there. I shook my head both yes and no. I let them know that it wasn't them. I just wanted to go home for the week-end.

Ever since the discovery of my toxemia/eclampsia, I had several long talks with God. My questions were, "What had I done to deserve this? Why now? Why was this happening?"

Nothing made sense about this condition. I took good care of myself. I had always been healthy. I felt absolutely fine the whole time and I didn't fit into the 'at risk' category.

The At Risk category included:

*First time mother

*Previous experience with gestational hypertension or pre-eclampsia

*Women whose mothers and sisters had pre-eclampsia

*Women carrying multiple babies; women younger than 20 or older than 40

*Women who had high blood pressure or kidney disease prior to pregnancy

*Women who are obese or have a BMI of 30 or greater

None of those applied to me.

This was my second child and the complications I had with my first pregnancy had nothing to do with hypertension or pre-eclampsia. Neither my mother nor my sister suffered any complications during pregnancy. I was 30 years old. I had no record of previous high blood pressure or kidney disease. When I became pregnant, I weighed 125 pounds on a 5'6" frame. I was much heavier now. Not only was I pregnant, but I had not been allowed to move around for months. Yes, I was angry at God. I was full of confusion, frustration, humiliation, guilt, and anger. You name the troubling emotion. I had it.

PIZZA PARTY

The nurses rearranged my room so I could lie on my left side and be able to see the television.

 My mom left and returned several hours later with a VCR and a stack of movies, as it seemed that I was going to be in the hospital for a while. Chad came later that afternoon.

The following day my grandmother spent much of the day with me. She read magazine articles to me and left me with a large stack of magazines and newspapers. My sister called to tell me that she and her husband were going to go pick up Channing at my parent's house. They would all be at the hospital around dinnertime. My room seemed to have a revolving door on it between family and nurses coming to check on me and help me. When

Dale, Alicia, Dylan, Summer, and Channing arrived, my room was full. Our families had always been close. It only seemed natural that they would come to try to lift my spirits.

We ordered pizzas to be delivered. Dale entertained the kids blowing up surgical gloves. We popped a movie in the VCR to entertain the kids while we ate our pizzas. Channing snuggled with me in bed. She loved playing with the remote for the bed causing it to move up and down.

After the movie, my sister asked Channing if she would like to go home with them and spend the night. She promised to bring her back to visit me the next day on Sunday.

Channing didn't mind spending the night with my parents as long as Dylan and Summer were there. She had never spent the night at my sister's house. I knew this was not going to work.

Dylan was nine, Summer was six, and Channing was four. Channing adored her cousins, but would never agree to spend the night with them. On this night, she surprised us all by saying, "Okay, I'll go home with you." I was shocked. My little girl was growing up.

Chad said that he would go over to their house for a little while and that way if she changed her mind, she could just go home with her dad. I think everyone was eager to get away from me and the hospital. I was so envious. All I wanted to do is be with them.

I awoke at two in the morning with pressure in my chest. I raised my bed a little and adjusted my pillows hoping that would help, and tried to get back to sleep. It seemed to be worse. I got up around 2:30 to take some antacid tablets. I thought the pizza must be causing this discomfort. It was probably heartburn. I took turns at pacing my room and resting. If I could just burp, everything should be okay. I thought that if I could go to the bathroom that might give me relief. There was still no change, nada, nothing. I felt very uncomfortable.

I was expecting the night shift nurse to make her rounds. In my previous visits, the nurse would wake me up between two and three to check my vitals. It was now almost 3:00 a.m. No one had come to my room. I was awake and hurting. I thought to myself, "This is stupid! You are in the hospital for a reason and are able to receive help."

I pushed the call button for the nurse. She answered, "Yes, Mrs. Moore."

"Just letting you know, I don't feel so good," I said.

"Okay, I'll be right there," I heard her reply.

While I waited for the nurse to arrive, I called Chad to let him know. Much to my surprise he actually answered. I figured I would have to leave a message. I told him that I had called the nurse because I didn't feel very good. "I am on my way there," he said.

I told him not to come, and that I felt it was just the pizza. I assured him that I would call back once the nurse left. All of a sudden, I cried, "Oh, my gosh, I am coming out of my skin!" Those were the exact words I said before I had Channing. I don't think we even said good bye.

The nurse arrived and checked me briefly. She left the room saying that she would be right back. All I remember after that is a room full of nurses. While they were trying to insert an IV line, I heard a stressed "Oh, shit," from one of the nurses. I'm not a doctor, but I'm pretty sure that's the term used for "not good".

Several hours later I woke up in a new room sitting doggie style on the bed vomiting in a tray.

Chad was holding the tray, and a nurse was rubbing my back. The nurse was gently saying, "It is okay, honey. You're doing just fine."

The doctor told Chad that he wanted to speak to him in the hallway somewhere between 5a.m. and 6 a.m. "Have you called the family yet? The doctor asked. Chad said that he hadn't called because he wanted to wait until everyone was awake. He told Chad, "Call the family. It isn't looking good. In fact, you need to be thinking about which one you want to save. It is likely that both Allison and the baby will not make it."

When I woke up sometime later, I was in a different room. Machines and tubes seemed to be connected to me everywhere. My mother was standing on my right side. She was holding my hand and stroking my hair. A nurse was on my left side watching monitors that were hooked up to me and the baby. Mother asked the nurse how I was doing. The nurse replied, "Not good. We are pumping 230 cc's of fluid in her an hour, and she is only putting out 30 cc's. That is the minimum to be alive. Her kidneys and liver are shutting down." The doctor had induced labor, inserted a catheter, and given me drugs to stop my seizures. I felt as if he had given me a drug to sleep. I was so very tired.

Mother was fighting to hold her tears back. She didn't want to frighten me more. I squeezed her hand and tried to assure her that I was okay. She was so emotional that she had to leave the room. She later told me that my face and body were so swollen that I was almost unrecognizable. She went to the rest room to get her emotions under control. Then she went to tell my dad and the rest of the family what the nurse had said. Most of the family had rushed to the hospital when they heard the danger the baby and I were in.

I woke up early in the afternoon with my whole extended family surrounding me. My grandparents, parents, aunt, uncle, sister, and Chad were all there. I thought they had spent the majority of the day in my room. My husband told me later that the doctor wouldn't let anyone stay in my room for very long except for him. It was very comforting to know my family was there, but I was so sick that I just wanted the delivery to be over.

The doctor called in a specialist to see me. He arrived around 2 p.m. in the afternoon. After he assessed my situation, he told me that I was doing well. Then he informed the nurses that if I hadn't had the baby by 3p.m. to prepare for a C-section. I didn't want a C-section, but I was ready to do anything to have my baby.

At 3:00 p.m., the specialist returned and announced that I was actually progressing very well. Then he said, "Let's give her until 4:00, if she has not had the baby by then, we will have to cut this baby out."

I didn't know it at the time, but what that meant was that my husband chose to save the baby. A nurse later explained, "If they would have cut you open, you would have bled out. Your vessels were like a soaker hose."

During the next hour, each contraction grew stronger, but the baby's heartbeat grew fainter. I finally got the nurses attention and told her that the baby didn't have a heartbeat. She replied, "Everything is okay, the baby's fine." It was time to start pushing when she informed me, "Don't worry, but we are going to have to resuscitate the baby."

That is exactly what I had been trying to tell them. I only pushed a couple of times when four pound Cassidy shot into the world at 3:59.

Only one minute to spare before the 4:00 time limit the doctor had set. The doctor even laughed saying he had to catch her like a football. The second she came out, the nurses were resuscitating her back to life. It seemed like forever before I heard her tiny cry. They immediately rushed her to the neo-natal intensive care unit (NICU). My room was now very quiet as everyone followed the baby. One nurse stayed with me. I remained in intensive care for the next 24 hours.

My doctor, who had ordered me to check into the hospital on Friday, had the week-end off. He came to visit me on Monday morning. I was glad to see him and thought the feeling would be mutual, but instead he scolded me like a child. He shook his finger at me and said, "If I would have let you go home, there is no way either one of you would have made it! You couldn't have made it to the hospital in time." He was mad at me to say the least.

 I sheepishly replied to him, "Yes, I know you were right."

He then let me know just how lucky I was to have him as my doctor. He was right about that, too.

LOOKING UP

On Monday evening, I was transported from the ICU back to my room on the third floor of the maternity ward. It was the floor for critical pregnancies. I was still hooked up to many IV's, and still had a catheter. A nurse was constantly coming into my room to take blood and check my vitals for several days.

Tuesday's routine was the same. I still hadn't been able to see or hold Cassidy. My doctor came by to check on me. This time he wasn't as upset with me. He explained that I had HELLP Syndrome. I had no idea what that meant. He explained that my enzyme and platelet levels were still far from where they should be. He informed me, "You will not be going home until these levels have greatly increased. Most women with eclampsia have their liver and kidneys start functioning normally immediately after they give birth. Your liver and kidneys are still not functioning properly. When we are able to get these all functioning normally, you can go home."

I grew up in a Christian home. We attended church every Sunday morning and evening as well as Wednesday nights. When I was very young I didn't like going because I was usually dragged outside and scolded for talking, lying down on the pew, or running up and down on the pew. (As I've mentioned before, I don't like to sit still.) Somehow some of the teachings filtered into my understanding. When your immediate family and your extended family are all strong Christians, faith and belief become a natural part of who you are.

I finally put all I had been taught about God to a test when I was about eight years old. My pet turtle named Yertle had been missing for weeks. Yertle lived in a large bowl in our utility room. We had looked all over the house for him. We knew he couldn't have gone too far. Now that several weeks had gone by I was really getting worried. Poor little guy hadn't had food or water. I was afraid he was dead. That evening when I went to bed I prayed, "Please, God, help me find my turtle before he dies." While I was praying I heard my mother call, "Allison! Allison!"

Whenever I heard my name called out like that it usually meant that I was in big trouble. My prayer changed to, "Please, God, don't let me be in trouble! Amen." Then I went to get my punishment.

My mom and dad were both standing in the den waiting for me. They motioned for me to follow them. A million things were going through my mind trying to figure out what I had done wrong. We arrived in the laundry room and there was Yertle. I was so excited that he was back. I was also amazed that God had answered my prayers while I was still praying. After that incident, I started behaving in church. I knew that God was really paying attention to everything I said or did.

My hospital room was at the end of the hall. I couldn't even see people coming and going. I felt so alone. Friends and family would come and visit, but they rarely spent much time with me. They wanted to see our baby, Cassidy. Of course, there were doctors and nurses coming into my room. I wanted to see my baby who was several floors downstairs. I was still hooked up to machines so I was stuck in the bed. The saddest part is that I felt abandoned by God. I know I should have been grateful for Cassidy and me just being alive, but everything in my life seemed to be going extremely bad.

Chad came to visit me on Tuesday night when he was able to get away from the stores. When he first arrived, he went to the NIC unit to check on Cassidy. The nurses told him that he had just missed her feeding, but if he was still there at 7p.m. to come back for her next scheduled feeding. The NIC unit would only allow a close family member to visit the infants for 30 minutes at a time. When you entered the NIC unit, there was a wash room where the visitor was required to scrub up to their elbows for at least one minute. The nurses and volunteers did a wonderful job of protecting their newborns.

Chad, in the meantime, came up and visited and had dinner with me. In a light hearted way, he commented about how bad I looked. He didn't mean it in a bad way, but rather as lighthearted teasing. I am sure he also was shocked that I was still bloated and swollen from head to foot. Some relatives didn't even recognize me. Normally these types of comments would have really bothered me. Since I couldn't get up to look in a mirror, I kind of appreciated it. I had always cared too much about how I looked. In fact, I wouldn't even go to the store without make-up. My eyes were normally very big, but appeared very small due to swelling. He had a good time joking about how much real estate my nose took up on my face. I wanted to snap back, but I just didn't have the energy to care. I could look at my urine bag and see I wasn't in good shape. There was still very little urine, and what was there was brown. I knew I didn't feel well, and that I wasn't recovering like I should. Even with toxemia, I should have recovered by Sunday at the latest.

It was nearing 7p.m., so Chad knew he had to leave to go to the NIC unit to feed Cassidy. I told him to give her a kiss for me, and told him to tell her that I couldn't wait to see her. I gave him two kisses, one for him and one for Cassidy. As he was leaving, I told him that I loved him, and to please tell Cassidy that I loved her too.

Not long after he left the room, I saw an angel come from the corner of the ceiling in my room. It swooped down over me carrying away the pain. Out loud, I said, "Thank you!" Another angel, then another, and another continued to swoop over me brushing away the pain with their wings. Each time

I cried out my thanks to them for helping me. I felt physically better as each angel swept over me taking my pain away. All of the angels were beautiful beyond description. My best description of them is beauty filled with pure love. Their garments were ivory in color, and flowed and fluttered like soft chiffon.

I had no idea what had just happened, but I knew that I felt dramatically better. It was as if an enormous weight had just been lifted from me. I wanted to get up and dance, but I couldn't because of all the contraptions connected to me. Chad returned and immediately asked,

 "What happened to you?"

I replied, "I feel so much better! What do you mean? Do I seem different?"

"I didn't mean anything negative," he replied, "It is just that you look like yourself again."

I began to cry because I knew he wouldn't believe what had just happened to me. Chad was a non-believer. He and I often argued over the Bible and religion. He asked, "What's wrong?

Why are you crying?"

"I know you're not going to believe me," I said, "but I had angels here with me the whole time you were gone. They were swooping over me and carrying away my pain."

He kept staring at me for what seemed like a long time. Then he shook his head and said, "I don't know what's happened, but you look amazing! Just remember that you are on a lot of drugs." That was his non-believing way to dismiss the miracle that had just occurred. It was now time for him to leave and go get Channing at my parent's house.

Around 10 p.m. that evening, I had another round of checkups from the nurses. When they walked in the room, they exclaimed, "Look at you!"

I replied, "I feel so much better." She checked my vitals and said, "You're doing good, hang in there." I was a little disappointed that she didn't unhook all the tubes from me. Then I thought maybe my husband was right. Maybe it was all the drugs messing with my mind.

My normal 3a.m. checkup arrived with the nurse taking several steps into my room and saying, "Oh, my God!" I quickly sat up and asked, "What's wrong?"

She stood there for several seconds, and then said, "No, this is great! This is awesome! You have flooded the room."

It took me a little while to realize that my catheter had exploded and flooded the room. I began to apologize profusely. I was completely embarrassed and humiliated.

"No, this is great," she replied as she continued to clean up my mess. I would have given anything to be able to do it myself.

The following day, Wednesday, I showed great progress and many of the tubes were removed.

Late in the afternoon, I was finally approved to meet my daughter for the first time in person.

Chad came so he could introduce me to our sweet baby girl. I expected it would be the other way around. As he wheeled me down the hall, doctors and nurses would look at me and shake their heads. Some would say, "You were so sick." I heard some whisper, "That is her." I almost felt like a celebrity in the maternity ward and in the halls on the way to the NIC unit. I couldn't escape comments about how sick I had been. I was feeling much better, and couldn't understand why I was getting all this attention.

I had given birth to Cassidy on September 19th, now it was the 22nd. After four days, I was finally going to meet her and hold her for the first time. The nurse handed Cassidy to me along with the smallest bottle I had ever seen. It looked like a tiny bottle from the pet store for a small animal. I informed the nurse that I wanted to breast feed. They allowed me the opportunity to try, but Cassidy had no response. They returned the miniature bottle to me, and instructed me on how to force her mouth open with my ring finger and pop the bottle into her mouth. They instructed me to continue stimulation of her chin and lips to encourage her to suck the bottle.

Cassidy had failure to thrive. She didn't have the strength or energy to do what is instinctive to most babies. She was so tiny and frail. Born at four pounds, she now weighed only three and a half pounds. I thought she was beautiful, and instantly fell in love with her.

Months later, I would look at pictures of her and realize that she looked like a baby bird. Her bones protruded out and her skin was loose, which was proof that she really needed those six weeks she was denied in the womb to fully develop.

Cassidy and I continued to get to know each other during the next several days. It was difficult to feel very comfortable, because we were still in two separate parts of the hospital. I was still only allowed thirty minutes with her at a time. We practiced at nursing, but continued with the bottle. Each day her bottle would be a little bigger with more ounces of formula. My enzymes and platelet counts also continued to show progress. By the week-end, Cassidy was back up to four pounds. The doctor announced that since we were both improving, we would be moved to a room where she and I could stay the night together. If all went well, they would decide on when we could go home.

Late Friday afternoon, a nurse took me to a room that was like a very nice hotel room. A short time later, Cassidy arrived in her small rolling baby bed. The nurse gave me a list of instructions along with a tutorial on how to care for a newborn. This wasn't my first child, but I knew they were just trying to help me in every way. I had to admit that I was very nervous knowing they were watching my every move to make sure that I was able to care for her. I wanted to go home so very much; however, I knew that I wouldn't have the luxury of having experts to help me at home. The nurses and doctors had done such a great job taking care of us. All the 'what if's' set in. What if I wasn't able to give her the care she needed? What if I couldn't care for a toddler and a preemie? What if I am not strong and healthy enough yet? What if I don't wake up when she cries?

That evening I enjoyed holding Cassidy and staring at her. I fed her before bedtime, put her down and fell asleep. Several hours later, I heard a squeak and figured it was a nurse opening the door to check on us. I sat up, but no one was there. I lay back down. I heard it again and sat up wondering if I had a mouse in the room. Then I realized that the squeak was Cassidy crying. She was a week old, and I had never heard her cry. Her little lungs could only produce a tiny little sound to let me know she needed me. I had always been a deep sleeper. Now I had to program my internal alarm clock to wake to just a tiny squeak.

ROUGH START

Cassidy and I successfully completed our night together in the hospital. They released us the following day. My mother and Channing met Chad in my room to help load up all the gifts, personal belongings, Cassidy, and me for the trip home. Mother was with Channing following Chad and me. As she was leaving the maternity ward, a nurse stopped her. She asked Mother, "Is that your daughter?" Mother nodded yes.   The nurse added, "She is one lucky girl. We just don't get them any sicker than she was. She was also lucky that when she delivered the baby, the doctor on call was a specialist with toxemia deliveries. A different doctor might have lost both of them."

We made it home and unloaded everything. Mother stayed for a while to cuddle her newest grandchild. Chad ran to the store to get needed supplies for Cassidy and me. When he returned he had sandwiches for dinner. After dinner, Channing went to her room to play. She was so happy to have our family all together again. Chad and I went outside to sit on the deck and relax. We took turns holding our tiny Cassidy. This had always been one of our favorite places to relax and visit with each other. That evening it felt even more special. I started to cry with joy. I was so thrilled to be home. After staying at my parents for four weeks, and a week in the hospital, it seemed like home was a distant memory. Chad and I discussed how extremely fortunate we were. My obstetrician saw and checked me the very day that my pressure tests showed danger. The next day, I was in the hospital when my numbers were at dangerous levels. The doctor on call was an expert in toxemia complications. The nurses were able to revive Cassidy when she was born. We felt so blessed that Cassidy and I both survived the delivery. As a family, we had escaped more financial trauma by being on Medicaid. Cassidy and I being in the ICU for a week would have been financially devastating. Our lives had been teetering on the edge of disaster, but we survived it all. I knew God had been holding us in his right hand protecting us.

Our enjoyable quiet time back at home literally came to a halt with loud screeching of tires and several loud bangs.   Channing came running from her bedroom meeting us running to her. We all quickly went to the front of our house. We met with our next door neighbors outside, where we found a car between our two houses. Two teenagers had taken the curve too fast. They had hit our mailbox, narrowly missed our cars in the driveway, and ran over a small tree. Luckily, the car stopped between our house and our neighbor's house without hitting either one. Thankfully, the boys in the car weren't hurt. I told Chad, "So much for a quiet peaceful first night at home."

A few days later Willa Faye, my mother-in-law, arrived from North Carolina. She couldn't wait to meet Cassidy. She was amazed how tiny Cassidy was. She was a little uncomfortable holding such a small, premature baby. We all felt that way because she looked so fragile.

Willa Faye and Chad went into the kitchen to start dinner, so I thought it would be a perfect time to get a shower. Babies made Chad nervous, especially when fussy, so I felt comfortable taking a break with his mother helping. Texas weather is unpredictable and many times, rain forecasts bring very little precipitation; however, we also can get some big ugly storms with high winds, lightning, hail, and downpours. I was enjoying my short amount of alone time, knowing that Chad and Willa Faye could handle the kids.

My retreat came to an abrupt end when the power went out followed by the pinging sounds of hail hitting the roof. I jumped out of the shower and threw on my clothes. I grabbed candles and lit them throughout the house. Dinner was on hold. We all sat in the glow of the candles not knowing how long the storm would last. We did get a good laugh at how fast I could take a shower and get dressed when I had to.

Thankfully, the power wasn't off for very long. It was just enough time for us to forget about dinner on the stove. I heard Willa Faye scream, "Chad, come help me! There's a fire in the kitchen!" I turned around to see flames coming from the untended pans on the stove. That was it! I was done. I laid my head on the table and started crying again. As crazy as it sounds, I wanted to go back to the hospital. Being back at home was supposed to be happy, calm, and life back to normal. I was totally stressed out and my nerves were frayed. I just couldn't take it anymore. Chad and Willa Faye put out the fire and no damage was done to the house. No more major incidents occurred, and our lives finally got back to normal.

Chad and I only allowed immediate family to hold and visit Cassidy. We wanted to give her more time to develop and gain immunities. Channing was totally fascinated with her tiny sister, and enjoyed showing her off. Jealously reared its ugly head when we started inviting friends over to visit. It didn't take long for her to figure out that if you can't beat them, join them. She got one of her baby dolls and copied everything I did for Cassidy. If I rocked Cassidy, Channing rocked her baby doll. When I bathed Cassidy, Channing bathed her doll. We would sit together and feed our babies.

When Channing first brought out her baby doll, I noticed that they seemed similar in size. I put Cassidy down, and asked Channing to lay her baby doll next to her. Cassidy was almost a month old and she was the same size as the doll. Over the next few months, Cassidy began to put on weight and grew much bigger. Each of her doctor's visits showed that she was on a normal growth track.

She was still small for her age but they explained that was because she was a preemie.

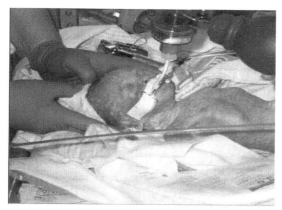

Cassidy at birth after being resuscitated.

Cassidy with Channing's baby doll.

NOT SO PERFECT

Not long after Chad and I learned that we were expecting Cassidy, we decided to sell our stores. The detour in front of one of our stores was still costing us business. My illness with Cassidy had taken a toll on Chad. I hadn't been there to help him run the stores, and we couldn't afford to hire more help. He was working seven days a week at full speed. We just couldn't see having a newborn baby and running three stores. We were hurting financially, but our family was suffering the most. The constant stress, and no time together, was wearing us all down.

After several months on the market, we received an offer from another Subway owner who had over 30 locations. The offer was going to be enough for us to pay my parents back everything we owed them, pay off the bank loan, and enough for Chad and I to make a small profit. The sale would close on the stores in November. The timing was going to be perfect for us. We realized that these transactions are often delayed. We believed the transactions would have closed by January, at the latest. November came and went with no closing. January came and went and we still had no closing. With each passing month our finances were getting worse.

February arrived with no mention of a closing date for the stores. It was Channing's birthday month. We planned a special party for her fifth birthday. She deserved a day that was all about her. Most of our attention had been going to the stores, my problem pregnancy, and her baby sister for almost a year. We invited friends and family for a cookout, cake, and ice cream. After the party, all the guests went home except for my sister and her family. I put Cassidy down for a nap, while Channing played with Dylan and Summer. When Cassidy woke up, Alicia went with me to get her fed and changed. I put Cassidy in her swing with some toys. While Cassidy was swinging, Alicia asked, "Does she always have her right hand in a fist?"

"I don't think so. Why do you ask?" I responded

Alicia told me of a friend of hers who had a baby a year older than Cassidy. He had a stroke when he was born that caused him to keep his hand in a fist all the time. I was offended that she brought this up. After all, I think I would know if there was something wrong with my child.

When Cassidy had her six month checkup, I mentioned Cassidy's right hand always being in a fist. Her pediatrician assured me she was perfectly fine, and not to worry. She stressed that since she was premature it would just take longer to do different things. I took great pleasure calling my sister to let her know that Cassidy was perfectly fine.

Over the next few months, I began to think that Alicia was right. Cassidy wasn't doing anything that a baby her age should be doing. When I would lay her on her stomach, she would never attempt to get on her hands and knees. Instead, she would roll over and push with her left hand to position herself on her bottom. If I put toys around her, she would only play with them with her left hand. Any task that required thought and effort would cause her to tighten her right fist. Her thumb was tucked in under her middle finger, holding down her ring finger.

One day, while reading the newspaper, I came across an article about a mother whose child had hemiplegia. Hemiplegia is a paralysis of one side of the body. It seemed to describe what I had observed in Cassidy to a "T". I cut out the article and put it in the diaper bag. On July 2nd, I took her for her nine month checkup. The nurse led us to the exam room. While she was checking Cassidy's weight, ears, and heart rate, I told her that I thought Cassidy had hemiplegia. I feel she must have told the pediatrician that she had a crazy Mom in room three. When the doctor arrived, she seemed to have a bit of an attitude. She asked rather irritated, "So, what do you think is wrong with Cassidy?" I replied, "I think she has hemiplegia." With a tilt of her head and a deep stare, she asked in a way that seemed to demean my opinion, "Now, what makes you think that?"

I handed her the article and pulled out a bunch of Cassidy's favorite toys. I laid them around her and told her to watch. Before long, Cassidy tightened her right fist, drew her right arm into her stomach and reached out with her left hand to grab her toys.

The doctor's eyes opened wide and then she said, "I think you are right. Hold on, I'll be right back. Deep down I was hoping that I was crazy, and she would dismiss my concerns as she had done previously. When she returned, she handed me some papers. She said that she had called Cooks Children's Hospital in

Fort Worth, and scheduled an MRI for Cassidy the following afternoon. All of a sudden, my world seemed to explode.

Our stores were scheduled to finally close on July 5th, which also happened to be my sister's birthday. It was 8 months past our original closing date. I expected this closing date to be cancelled just as all previous closings had been. Selling the stores had been a nightmare. The man buying our locations bought and sold stores all the time, so he had the process down to an art. He knew that once the contract was signed there was little the seller could do, and he knew how to manipulate the sellers into desperation. That was exactly where Chad and I were: we were desperate. All of our profit was gone. The bank, holding the loan on our stores, had been sold twice since we had bought them. Our new bankers were not acquainted with us and treated us and with no compassion or understanding. Instead of working with us until the sale was final, they were putting more pressure on us.

I was a nervous wreck on July 3rd when I took Cassidy to the hospital for an MRI. I prayed that the results would be good. I needed solutions on how we could get her to use her right side.

On this day, the stores were not on my mind. All I could think about was Cassidy. When we arrived at the hospital and checked in, they presented us with a stack of paperwork. We signed, giving the hospital permission to perform the procedure and administer anesthesia. When I heard our name called, I got up with Cassidy and waved to Chad. The nurse shook his head and said, "You can't go back with her." He assured me that everything would be okay and that he would come and get us when she woke up. I nervously returned to my seat next to Chad in the waiting room.

Not long after they took Cassidy back for the MRI, my cell phone rang. It was our attorney. I showed Chad who it was and we quickly went outside to take the call. Our attorney gave us a long list of things that we needed to bring to closing on July 5th.

I figured he was calling to cancel as he had so many times before. I told him that we were at the hospital and reminded him that the next day was the 4th of July. There was no way any of the places would be open to get the items on the list. When we hung up with the attorney, Chad and I discussed an action plan. I called my mother, who was already babysitting Channing. I asked if we could bring Cassidy over once the appointment was over. Of course, Mom agreed. She and Dad were as ready for the stores to close as we were, if not more so. They had co-signed for the loan on the stores and their whole life savings was on the line.

Chad and I had gone to the hospital in separate cars. As soon as we hung up with the attorney, Chad left to start attacking the list of things needed for the closing. I returned to wait for Cassidy to be released. I felt so frustrated. I couldn't help Chad get everything done that had to be done. I couldn't help Cassidy. All I could do was sit, wait, and pray.

After several hours, they called my name and took me back to meet with a doctor. They explained that her MRI showed abnormality to the left side of her brain, which affected the parietal and temporal lobes of her brain. The doctor felt she would never

65

be able to walk or talk. I was stunned and numb.
How could that be? My precious Cassidy had such a
hard path ahead.

On the drive to my mother's house, I found my
thoughts going in a million different directions. Is
Cassidy going to need a wheelchair, or maybe leg
braces? Are we going to have to learn sign
language? Then my thoughts would switch to the
stores, and what I needed to do in order to
accomplish the tasks required for the closing. Then
back to Cassidy; will she ever be able to drive, dress
herself, and what about dating? My thoughts were
spinning out of control. This was all too much for
one day. My stress level had skyrocketed!

Cassidy was still foggy from the anesthesia when I
dropped her off with my mother. I quickly left to get
my half of the list completed. I told mom that I
would fill her in later on the test results. It took me
until 5p.m. to get all the bank and tax records
together, and then I returned to Mom's to pick up
the girls. I had been so busy all day that I had
forgotten to eat. While I filled Mom in on the day's
events, I grabbed a yogurt bar. I thought hunger
was part of my shaky, sick feeling. The stress of the
day's events sure didn't help matters.

I quickly loaded the kids in the car and left to meet up with Chad at a friend's house for a cook-out. On the way over to Vicky and Mick's house, I began to feel sick at my stomach. I thought it must be my nerves and not eating much all day. After visiting with our friends for a short time, I began to feel worse. I quietly slipped inside the house to lie down on the couch for a little while. It was hard to stay there when I could hear everyone outside talking, laughing and having a good time. After a short time, I decided to go back outside and join in on the fun. Once I stood up it hit me. I made a dash to the restroom and threw up. Each time I thought I was done, I was wrong.

I heard the kids running down the hall. I opened the door and yelled out for Channing. I told her to go get her dad, and tell him that I was sick. Chad quickly packed up the kids and handed me some plastic bags to use on the way home. I continued to be sick all the way home and most of the night. I woke up the next morning with severe pain on my right side. Each step I took brought more pain. I made my way to the deck where Chad was drinking his coffee. He asked me what I wanted to do. I thought that maybe I was just hurting from throwing up for so long. It was the 4th of July, and I knew that if I pushed my way through the day and didn't get better, the emergency room would be packed with holiday accidents. Around 9 a.m., we dropped off the girls with my parents, and headed to the emergency room. I hoped that I just had a stomach virus and would be sent home. We had plans to celebrate the 4th with friends at Lake Grapevine that afternoon.

After I got checked into the hospital, they ran several tests and took x rays. By early afternoon, the doctor came in to consult with me. He explained that there were no tests that could prove appendicitis. His opinion was that I had all the symptoms, and the tests had not shown another cause for the pain and vomiting. He recommended an immediate appendectomy. By late afternoon, I was in surgery having my appendix removed. After I woke from surgery, the doctor confirmed that I had a bad appendix that was on the verge of rupturing. That night I looked out my window in the hospital and watched the fireworks show at the Ballpark in Arlington where the Texas Rangers play baseball. It was definitely a day and a night to remember.

The following day, July 5th, was my sister's birthday, and our stores were scheduled to close. My name and Chad's name were on all the legal documents which required both of our signatures. My parents went with Chad to the closing since I was in the hospital. Our attorney called my room and asked me to give my mother Power of Attorney to sign all the papers on my behalf. Then he put me on a conference call to finish out the closing.

I was released from the hospital on July 6th with instructions to not lift anything heavy for six weeks. I had a nine month old baby that I couldn't pick up. I was physically, mentally, and emotionally spent. I knew that Cassidy had a stroke that would affect the rest of her life. I had missed so much. I was not there for Cassidy after the MRI, the 4th of July celebrations, my sister's birthday, and the closing of our stores. The closing of the stores gave me a sense of relief in a way, but also left me with a feeling of failure. I felt that I had been a burden on my whole family for several years. For the first time in my life, I felt that I would be better off dead. I had reached the end of my rope and I was ready to let go and call it quits.

LIFE IS NOT FAIR

Lots of prayer and thought brought me back to reality. Cassidy's stroke meant that she would need me even more. Life would be more difficult for Chad and Channing without me to help carry my share of the load. Life had been extremely hard and stressful, but we were all still alive, and we loved each other. I had to just take life one day at a time, and hang on the best that I could.

Cassidy's pediatrician recommended that we see the orthopedic doctor at Cooks Children's Hospital in Fort Worth. The orthopedic doctor looked over her chart and examined her. He then informed me that there was no cure, but recommended physical and occupational therapies. Before we left his office he asked about her eyesight. I shrugged and said, "I think she sees just fine." He grabbed a long stick with a feather hanging off the end. He dangled the feather around the back of her head, and brought it slowly along her left side. She quickly turned her head to the left when she saw the feather. He then returned the feather back around to appear on her right side. She didn't acknowledge the feather until it was directly in front of her. He repeated the test several more times, and each yielded the same results. I was told that Cassidy had no peripheral vision on her right side. We left the orthopedic doctor with a referral to see and eye specialist for further testing.

After a few weeks, we met with the ophthalmologist. He confirmed that she had no peripheral vision in her right eye. The doctor drew an oval on a piece of paper and said, "Most of us see like this." Then he blacked out a quarter of the oval and said, "This is what Cassidy sees." I asked if there was a procedure or therapy that could restore full vision.

The doctor responded that there was nothing that could be done to restore her vision. He tried to assure me that she would learn to look to her right and manage quite well. That explained why she bumped into people and things all the time. I had thought it was because she was an uncoordinated toddler.

We started physical and occupational therapy sessions twice a week through Cooks Children's Hospital and continued until our benefits ran out a few months later. Their therapist told me about a program we had available in Texas called ECI (Early Childhood Intervention). Through ECI, a therapist would come to our home once a week, free of charge, to work with Cassidy until the age of three. That program was such a blessing. There was no way we could afford therapy through the Cooks Hospital network with no insurance.

When we sold the stores, we were able to settle with the bank for less than we owed. We were still left with a tremendous amount of personal debt. Chad and I tried to calculate a plan to get out of debt, and to get back on our feet. Our finances were so bad. Even if we worked hard and did without, it would take many, many years to dig our way out of this deep hole. We decided to contact an attorney to see if we would qualify for bankruptcy. When we called to set an appointment to consult with the attorney, he gave us a list of documents to bring to our appointment. He explained that the laws had changed in the last few years, and it was almost impossible to qualify. The first appointment was free, so we figured we had nothing to lose.

We arrived for our appointment with the attorney with our tax records, bank statements, and monthly bills. The attorney reviewed all of our records and informed us that he had good news and bad news for us. He said the good news was that we qualified for filing bankruptcy. The bad news was that he had never seen it this bad. That meant that for the first time ever we were "over" qualified. We were able to file Chapter 7. That wiped out all debt. We weren't proud or happy to file Chapter7. In fact, it was yet another humiliating experience.

Chad and I had tried to prepare Channing for what it would be like to have a little sister. We had told her how important it was to be kind and loving with her. She would get to help us with the new baby by getting toys, diapers, bottles, and pacifiers. We thought as our new baby grew that she would want to emulate her big sister. They would have fun playing together and grow close. Channing felt the normal jealously after Cassidy was born, but it didn't get better. Cassidy needed more help than the average baby. All the trips to doctors and therapists and daily talks of Cassidy's progress only made matters worse. We tried to include Channing, and stress to her the importance of being a helper. Channing had always been quiet and mature for her age. She had been accepting of the new responsibilities that came with being a big sister. She was artistic, analytical and intuitive. She seemed to always see the big picture and understood most situations. It always amazed me that when given the opportunity to receive something, she would turn it down. She would reply that she didn't need it. I wanted to reward her because she had been such a good helper, and needed some special attention.

Channing was now six and a half, and had almost finished kindergarten. I thought as a special treat that I would take her to the beauty salon and get her hair done for the first time. She had beautiful long, naturally curly, blonde hair that I hated to cut. I thought cutting it would be a good idea to make her feel more special and grown up. The hair stylist gave her an adorable bob hair style. Family, friends, and teachers commented on her cute new hair style for weeks. She was showered with much needed attention. It seemed to even give her more self-confidence and spunk. Once the attention died down, she tried to find a way to get us to focus on her in other ways.

One evening I prepared the tub to bathe the girls. I knocked on Channing's door and told her to get in the tub. I went to get Cassidy ready to put in the tub with Channing. I would always bathe Cassidy first, dry her, wrap her in a towel, and take her to Chad to dress her in her pajamas. Then I would go back to help bathe Channing and wash her hair, and get her ready for bed. When I got to the bathroom, Channing was having fun playing. When I reached over to wash her hair, I noticed her hair felt different. There was almost no hair on her head on the side that faced the wall. I felt sick. "Oh, my goodness, what have you done to your hair? Where is your hair?" I cried out to her. When I turned her around, I could see that the hair on her left side was only about two inches long. I asked her in frustration and anger, "Did you cut your hair?"

She answered very innocently, "No".

I replied, "Oh really? Then what happened?"

She finally admitted that she had cut her hair, and it was in her room. I didn't know whether to laugh or cry. She looked so pitiful trying to cover up the huge spot on her head that was almost bald. She was sorry, sad, and afraid. Kids really know how to get our attention. I looked all around her room, but couldn't find any hair. Finally, I looked behind her closet door. There I found a stack of throw pillows in the corner. Under the pillows was her Easter hat filled with scissors and a pile of blonde curls. When I returned to the bathroom, she cried, "Mom, it isn't fair. Everyone does everything for Cassidy. No one helps me."

"Do you know why we do everything for her?" I asked.

"Yes, because she can't use her right hand," she answered with frustration.

I sat down and said, "I want you to take your right hand and put it behind your back and try to do everything with only one hand. Then tell me how unfair your life is. Do you understand?"

I got her out of the tub, dried her off, and wrapped her in a towel. I told her, "I am very unhappy with what you did, but I love you very much. Tomorrow I will take you to the hair stylist and see if she can give you a new hair style to cover up the mess that you have made.

But, you have to promise that you won't ever cut your own hair again. "

I realized that Channing would have to help her sister for years to come. If she understood more of what Cassidy had to deal with, maybe it wouldn't be as hard on her. Empathy and not sympathy is what I was hoping for her, so she would feel better about helping her sister.

We had high hopes for Cassidy to improve. She had already proven some doctors wrong by learning to talk and walk. She had been slower to develop these skills because of her stroke and being six weeks premature. We knew that she had difficulty with these skills, but she was doing them. Her right ankle and toes were locked, so walking was slow. There had been no improvement in the use of her right arm or hand. We had been given no hope for her to be doing as well as she was. We had hope for more improvement because children's brains change so dramatically the first few years of life. They have a better chance to learn new ways of doing things because everything in life is new to them. We also wanted to help her as much as possible while she was young because older children can often be cruel. We were willing to try anything that would give her a more normal life.

We continued Cassidy's therapy sessions with ECI, but the time was approaching where she would be too old for their services. About six months before Cassidy's third birthday, her ECI therapist told me about several programs that she thought would benefit her. One of the programs was Kooken, a school in Arlington, designed to help children with special needs. It helped to prepare them to be mainstreamed in public schools. There was a waiting list, and every child had to test into the school to prove they needed special attention due to a disability. We needed to go ahead and start the process. The other program was Scottish Rite Hospital for Children in Dallas. They treated children with special needs free of charge, but required a recommendation from a Mason.

Cassidy was accepted for Kooken. We were thrilled that she had this wonderful opportunity. On her third birthday, the school bus arrived to pick her up for a half day of school.   She was scared and cried, squirmed, and screamed when we put her on the bus. I remained firm and reassured her that everything would be okay. I reminded her that she would be going to school just like her big sister. My strength and resolve dissolved when I reached our front door. I couldn't believe that I had just put my sweet, three year old Cassidy on a bus with strangers she didn't know. I prayed that I was doing the right thing for her. We had always tried to protect our girls, but especially Cassidy. She needed our protection, but it was difficult to know when we were protecting her too much. Being the parent of a special needs child was so hard. All parents question themselves, but knowing what is best for a special needs child is much more difficult. We don't truly understand all their challenges. Everything in life is different for them, and we can't truly relate to what they are experiencing.

Kooken was a wonderful school for Cassidy. She grew to love it, and only cried when she had to miss school. Not long after she started at Kooken, our friends Vicky and Mick invited our family over to watch a Cowboy's football game and a cook out. Vicky and Mick had a great place for entertaining. They lived on three acres with horses, four wheelers, trampoline, playground, and pool. It was perfect for the whole family to kick back and relax. When we arrived, we saw that Margaret, one of their neighbors, was joining us. As usual, the men either hung out at the grill or in front of the TV. The women usually gathered out on the deck or in the kitchen. Margaret, Vicki, and I sat on the deck and chatted about what was going on in our lives. I told them that Cassidy had started school at Kooken, and that her therapist had also recommended Scottish Rite Hospital. I mentioned that we really wanted her to be able to be accepted there, but we didn't know anyone who was a Mason. Without a letter of recommendation from a Mason, she had no chance at all to go there. Margaret quickly said, "My dad is a Mason!"

Margaret was only an acquaintance, and by no means were we close friends. I certainly didn't know her parents. She immediately called her dad and told him about Cassidy. Then she asked if he would write a letter of recommendation for her. He agreed, and gave Margaret a list of information that she needed to get from me. Within a few weeks, we had a letter of referral and an acceptance to Scottish Rite Hospital. We felt so blessed to have additional help for Cassidy.

Chad and I really enjoyed spending time with Vicki and Mick. They were very strong evangelical Christians. Although Chad was not sold on religion, it was good to have friends to help back me up and give their own prospective. Vicki, Mick, and Margaret had each been married before. Each of them had experienced their share of problems and tragedy. Mick had three children from a previous marriage, two grown daughters, and a son who had died at birth. He and Vicki had three children together. Their oldest daughter was born with one lung and her heart on the wrong side. She was only expected to live around five years, but surprised all the doctors by doing well and flourishing. When their youngest daughter was taken to the doctor for her one year checkup, a tumor was discovered around the lower part of her spine. She went through chemotherapy, radiation, and surgery. She became a star basketball player in school, healthy, and happy. Thankfully, their youngest son had no major health issues.

Margaret and her husband had a large blended family. They loved and supported each other and all the children. They owned a second house on the river where they spent a lot of time in the summer. They loved the river and water skiing. One day when Margaret's husband was skiing, he fell the wrong way, breaking his neck. He was paralyzed for life. They stayed together for many years, until he chose to divorce her.

The fact that Chad was not a Christian never stopped Vicki and Mick from praying over Cassidy. I was brought up in a very conservative church where church services and prayer were quiet and subdued. We prayed aloud before meals, and alone in bed at night, at times, silent prayers during the day that only God and I knew about. I wasn't used to their very public, (no matter what you are doing), kind of prayer. They would often start praying aloud in a group with a beer in their hand.

Vicki and Mick would lay hands on Cassidy and thank God in advance for her healing. I was happy with their prayers, because I had seen miracles with their two daughters. I appreciated any and all prayers. I would have traded places with Cassidy if I could. I just wanted her to be normal, and be able to live a full healthy life.

Mick was particularly sweet to Cassidy. He called her either "Cassidy girl" or "precious child of God." Sometimes he would put it all together. He would say, "Come and see me, Cassidy girl, you precious child of God." He did this so often that sometimes when people met her, and asked her name, she would reply, "I am Cassidy Moore; a precious child of God." What a beautiful message for any child to have ingrained in their mind.

GOD, WHAT ELSE COULD GO WRONG?

I should know better than to ask God that question because he always shows me. When 2000 rolled around, we had high hopes that the New Year would bring a change in our stress levels. I knew from all that had happened to us in the last few years that I never wanted to be unemployed or self-employed again. Cassidy was growing and my health was better. We felt that our lives could start moving forward without so much stress.

We had always been a tight knit family. Grandparents, parents, kids, and grandkids gathered frequently for birthday parties, lunches, and special occasions. Frequent phone calls filled us in on all the news in everyone's daily lives. We all knew that my grandfather, Paw Paw, had Alzheimer's. He could still function fairly well with Granny watching over him. Then Granny started worrying over a multitude of ailments that she was experiencing. The list of symptoms grew from pain in her back to a list that would fill a notebook page. She was taken to every kind of specialist that was suggested. None of the doctors could diagnose her. My mother and aunt even took her to a psychologist, a psychiatrist, and finally to a neurologist. No medications or therapies could stop her rapid deterioration. Mother or Aunt Virginia went to Granny and Paw Paw's house almost every day to check on them. We were all so worried about her, and felt helpless.

At the end of 2000, Granny was not her old self, and my parents were not acting like themselves. My sister and I noticed that our parents were very cool to each other, which was very strange behavior for them. They had been married for 40 years, and rarely had an argument. When Alicia and I asked what was wrong, we were told that everything was fine, or that it was just stress over taking care of Granny and Paw Paw. We decided to mind our own business, and stay out of it.

The beginning of the new year, 2001, started with a meeting with Mom and Dad. They called and invited my sister and me over for a talk. They admitted that they were in the middle of major problems in their marriage. They were not planning to divorce, but thought they should explain why their behavior had been so strange. They told us of the problems they were trying to work out, and wanted us to know they loved us. This news was such a shock. We thought everything had always been great between them. We could only remember two big arguments the whole time we were living at home with them. No one in our home had even raised their voices. No yelling, no cursing, no fighting in our childhood memories. Alicia and I were upset and sad. There was nothing that we could do, but be there for them.

Our family really believes in the marriage vows. Problems have to be addressed and worked out. That isn't always easy or pleasant. We just had to have faith that they could get through this. Mom and Dad had drifted away from the church a few years before, because they couldn't find one they liked. They just gave up looking for one after we moved to Arlington.

We had moved to different cities many times because of Dad's job, and we had always been able to find a church home that we all agreed to. They had just quit trying, and gave up several years before. To repair their marriage they decided that they had to find a church and rebuild their relationship with God. They found one that not only blessed them and their marriage, but our whole family.

I knew every family had problems. Some people had more problems, and far worse than ours had been, but I was feeling guilty that I had caused a lot of their stress. The financial strain that the stores had put on Chad and me and my parents, my problem pregnancy, Cassidy's health problems, my surgery, and my grandparents health issues were a lot to deal with on a daily basis. They hadn't had a break from serious problems for years. That didn't even include issues from Dad's side of the family. It was a shame that when they needed faith the most, they had withdrawn from church. We all had withdrawn from church. That old saying fit us: "When you feel God isn't near, who moved away?" I knew we had all let the world get in the way of our relationship with God. God was always in our lives, but we weren't putting God first.

Mom and Dad found a wonderful church. They were so thrilled with the church and the minister, Randy Frazee, that they looked forward to the next service. They couldn't wait to tell us all about the weekly sermons. We were so thrilled by their enthusiasm that we decided to go try it ourselves. Within a few months, our whole family was attending. We were so amazed that each sermon seemed to be speaking directly to our family. Many Sundays, the sermons touched us so deeply that we would leave with tears in our eyes. One example of a particularly touching sermon was about the minister's son. His teenage son had been born without his left arm. He told how he had been angry with God about his disability. He told how he would have gladly given his left, dominate arm to his son, if it was possible. Then he told us of how much his son had accomplished with only one arm. He had played sports, drums, and even learned how to tie his own shoes. In the end, he knew that God had given his son everything he needed to fulfill God's purpose in his life. That sermon took a huge weight off my shoulders. I knew that Cassidy was perfect in God's sight. I had to let go and let God.

Granny's health continued to decline rapidly. Everyone in the family was baffled at how to help her. Doctors either said they had no idea what was wrong, or they said it was all in her head. In a way, it turned out to be all in her head. It was an extremely rare neurological disease. In her last few months of life, it was tentatively diagnosed as corticobasal ganglionic degeneration. One reason the doctors couldn't diagnose her was that hers had been so aggressive. Most people have it for six to eight years. Granny's only lasted a little over two years.   By the end of 2001, she couldn't communicate, but only mumble one or two words at a time or makes sounds. She was curled up in a semi fetal position most of the time. Only her eyes could communicate with us.

 She showed joy when she first saw us walk in, but most of the time we only saw fear and confusion. The last few months of her life she wanted babies around her. We bought fabric with babies on it to make her blankets, and baby dolls for her to hold. These seemed to bring her peace. To have her life taken from her by such a humiliating and debilitating illness seemed cruel.

After hospice was called in for her, she couldn't communicate at all. I was good at holding her hand and visiting with family in her room. I wasn't good at saying my final good-bye. The hospice nurse encouraged us to all say our final words that we needed to say because her time was very short. She informed us that hearing is one of the last senses to be lost, so Granny should hear us. I was having a really difficult time with my final words. The hospice nurse called me over to her and handed me a pamphlet that explained the dying process and patted my arm.

The hospice nurse said, "This is the day she has lived her whole life for."

That statement was so true and changed my perspective on everything. If anyone had lived their life preparing for eternal life with our Father, it was my grandparents. I leaned over and said, "Granny, I love you so much, and I just want you to know that it's okay to go home. We will all be okay and we will take good care of Paw Paw." She went home around 4am the following morning.

Paw Paw and Granny had always been strong Christians that really lived their faith. They were happy, successful, and loving. They had set a good example on how to be involved in the church, work hard, to be generous with time and money, and most of all to love. Paw Paw was always in a suit and tie, unless he was playing golf. When he came home from work, the dress clothes stayed on until bedtime. Granny never left the house without every hair in place and looking her best. She was attentive to weight, hair, make-up, clothing, and accessories every time she left the house. She always looked elegant. They both believed you should always present your best self. They felt you had to earn people's respect by your actions and your appearance. It didn't seem fair that these people, who were the personification of a lady and a gentleman, would spend their last days with no control over their minds and bodies. Paw Paw didn't even realize that Granny was dying. She only weighed about 80 pounds the last few months, and couldn't even swallow. He kept telling us that she was just fine. When Granny died, Paw Paw's alzheimers had progressed to the point he shouldn't be left alone. The sad decision was made to move him to an alzheimer's facility. Our patriarch, who was a leader, an elder in the church, and had owned a successful business, was losing himself and his dignity.

The next year, 2003, my other grandfather, Pops, died. He was in a bowling league with my dad. One morning while bowling, he grabbed his stomach and said to call an ambulance. He was rushed to the hospital and tests were done. A few hours later he was told that he needed surgery, his abdominal aneurism was about to burst. He needed immediate surgery, but no one in The Fort Worth or Dallas area could do the procedure. He would have to be flown to Houston. That could give him a little more time.

Pops refused the surgery because he couldn't stand the thought of going through so much pain for just the possibility of a short time added to his life. He also didn't want to give up his independence, or be a burden to his family. That night after we had all had an opportunity to give him our love and to tell him good bye, he passed away. His passing was sad, but he was able to work, fish, bowl, and enjoy life until his last day on earth.   He wanted to live to 90, and he almost made it, dying at 89.

That same year, we did have some good news when my sister gave birth to their third child Jadyn. The news of the pregnancy, however, did bring my sister and brother-in-law much panic. Both Alicia and Dale were turning 40 and thought they were through having kids.

They had their first child Dylan in 1990. Three years later they had Summer, and thought their family was complete. For 10 years they discussed and sometimes argued which one of them would get "fixed". I'm still not sure which one of them won or which of them lost. In a way I think both of them lost because my sister had to endure nine months of pregnancy and the pains of labor. Dale, however, joined in the group of guys in what we had dubbed "The V Club" and got a vasectomy. We all won because none of us could imagine life without their daughter, Jadyn.

GROWING UP

After faithfully attending church for three years as a family, Chad came to know Christ. He said it hit him one afternoon at home like a bolt of lightning that brought him to his knees. He told me of an overwhelming feeling of unconditional love and power; the kind of power that gives you the ability to heal someone by laying hands on them.   He felt the power of Jesus was in him and that he could actually use it to heal, and help others. I could understand, because I had that same feeling from time to time. I have had times when I feel that Jesus is sitting right next to me. Then there are the times when I feel he is far, far away.

Soon we learned that Randy Frazee, our minister, was leaving our church to teach at a church in Chicago. Our whole family was devastated. We loved our church services and our church family, but especially our minister. Our whole family went to services and sat on the same row. After services, we would go to Mom and Dad's house for lunch.

One Sunday after lunch, Mother asked if anyone wanted to be baptized by the minister before he left for Chicago. Channing quickly raised her hand, and Chad nodded his head in agreement.

 A few weeks later we all arrived at our minister's home. We went to his back yard pool, where he baptized Chad, now 41, and Channing, 10, in his hot tub. Our minister spoke of his father, and how he had always struggled that he had never come to know Jesus. He told Channing how special it was that her father had come to know our Father in Heaven and what a special gift it was for him to share this experience with her. They had given their lives to Jesus in Baptism, together.

After Cassidy completed Kooken School for special needs children, she entered elementary school in our neighborhood. She continued both physical and occupational therapy through the public school system. We also continued appointments at Scottish Rite Hospital. I had considered discontinuing treatments because each time I took her they would say, "Okay, now we need to see her again next year." Each year I took her back in hopes of something new being discovered that would help her.

In 2011, her neurologist suggested the drug Artane. He felt it would help to relax her right hand and help to control her drooling. Cassidy was eleven and very embarrassed when she drooled at school. Since she didn't have any feeling on her right side, she wouldn't feel that she was drooling. She only became aware of it when drops would fall on her books or classwork. Of course, she thought everyone around her noticed it.

Before issuing the prescription for Artane, Cassidy's doctor sent us to the third floor to meet with a physical therapist for testing. The testing is known as the Assisting Hand Assessment (AHA). They videotaped her playing a game. The game consisted of a game board with cards of different colors set in the middle of the board. The cards gave instructions on where to go and what to do once you get there. The therapist had several different objects set out to the side. Some of the instructions required Cassidy to cut paper, open containers, wind up a toy, and put on a head band. Each task was very difficult to do with only one hand. The therapist then carefully observed the video and scored her on a scale of 22-88 on categories such as: orients objects, stabilizes by weight or support, grasps, and moves forearm. There were even more categories to be scored. Cassidy scored a 43 on her first test, and we decided to start the Artane. I didn't notice any change in her right hand, but it did seem to reduce the drooling. We went back to Scottish Rite after four months and they retested her. Her score went down to 42. The therapist said that any score within a four point range is considered to be no change. We continued with the Artane for about a year until we decided to discontinue its use. She never liked taking it because she said it tasted bad, and she had to take it three times a day.

When Cassidy was a toddler, she loved to play with her baby dolls and push them around the house in her toy stroller. Although she had more trouble doing things, it never stopped her from trying. Her older sister gave her the inspiration to try to do everything that she did. But as a pre-teen, Cassidy just wanted to "veg" out in her spot on the couch with a remote in her good hand. When I would try to encourage her to find something fun to do, she would reply,

"No, everyone in the neighborhood is outside on bicycles, scooters, or climbing trees. I'm pretty much left by myself watching them have fun."

When kids would come over to play, she would want them to sit on the couch with her watching movies or the Disney channel. The kids would soon get bored and go home.

I had always told Cassidy that she could do whatever she put her mind to, but I was wrong. I would show her videos online of others who were missing limbs, or were disabled in some way. They still accomplished amazing things with determination. I would forget that her disability was in the brain. Her right side had never worked because the wiring had never worked properly. That part of her brain was damaged at birth and had never functioned. If someone loses an arm, they often learn to use their feet and toes to compensate. People who have lost an arm or a leg still have nerves and muscles that are functioning. If someone loses an arm or a leg they can get a new limb and learn to use it. The stroke she had in utero caused her brain to not be able to connect properly to her right side. No matter how hard she worked the nerves would not function. When you don't use a limb, the bones and muscles don't grow as they should. Now we were noticing that her right hand was smaller.   It is so heartbreaking to know that your child can't do the fun things that go with childhood. It is even more heartbreaking to know they will always have difficulties doing the everyday things that we all take for granted.

Cassidy never wanted to attend her friend's birthday parties, or go to sleepovers because she was uncomfortable with other people having to help her. She wanted to do things on her own. She needed help with her hair, putting toothpaste on her toothbrush, showering and going to the bathroom. She would often get stuck when changing clothes with her right arm tangled in the clothing.

When Cassidy was in second grade, her big sister, Channing, was entering junior high school. Channing became interested in tennis and started taking lessons. Her older cousins, Dylan and Summer, were superstars in high school basketball. It seemed at every family dinner and function the conversation centered on their sports. Attention was lavished on the teenager's fun and success in their sports. That definitely caught Cassidy's attention. She began to question everyone in the family, "What sport do you think I would be good at?"

We suggested several sports that we thought she might be able to participate in, but all were rejected. We knew that any of the sports we suggested would be almost impossible for her to accomplish. No one wants to be told that you can't or shouldn't participate in anything. This was very disheartening to us, but especially to her. Cassidy didn't want to take lessons because she didn't want to draw attention to her disabilities. She had always done a great job of hiding her hand and arm from people. It was only natural that she just wanted to fit in and not be different.

Channing and Cassidy had always had a strong desire to impress their teachers. They worked to do their best in every subject, and to be kind to their peers. Cassidy never liked physical education, but she did her best. The teachers were understanding and kind to her, but she dreaded P.E. class anyway. The only day of the year that she would cry going to school was field day. The one day that is designed for kids to have fun, filled her with much anxiety. She feared that others would judge her athletic abilities. She would be disappointed because she never received a ribbon.

At the end of her fourth grade year, Cassidy was handed a letter from one of her teachers asking her to be a "special friend". She came home from school that day floating on cloud nine. She couldn't contain her excitement as she told me that only the popular kids were asked to do this.

"You must be popular, too", I told her.
She replied emphatically, "No, Mom! I am not popular. You can only be a special friend when you're in the fifth and sixth grade, and if a teacher puts in a recommendation for you."

I gave her a big hug and exclaimed, "Congratulations! What is the job description of a special friend?"

 She explained that special friends help the children with special needs in the mornings and afternoons to get on and off the bus. They assist them in getting to their classrooms and out to meet the bus. This was especially great for Cassidy to be given these responsibilities.

Her teachers trusted her, a girl with disabilities, to assist other kids with disabilities. Instead of focusing on what she couldn't do, her teachers were focusing on what she could do.

Cassidy took her job as a special friend very seriously. She quickly fell in love with all the kids in the special needs program, and they all fell in love with her. It was then that she decided that she wanted to be a special needs teacher when she grew up. Cassidy flourished knowing that she was helping others. The new responsibilities helped her to feel needed and appreciated. Instead of being helped, she could be a helper. She also now knew there were things that she could do, and do well, with her disabilities. Of course, it helped getting positive recognition from the kids and her teachers. Our whole family could see her confidence grow.

Cassidy really needed this because school was so hard for her. Everything was harder, and doing her homework took up every evening until bed time. Cassidy was slower to get her work done, not only because of slower physical tasks, but also, because her brain had to work twice as hard to decipher the questions and problems. We would all wind up tired and frustrated, and therefore, we dreaded doing homework.

At her graduation from elementary school, one of the special needs teachers approached her. She handed Cassidy a beautiful James Avery heart necklace. Then she pulled out her own matching necklace. She told Cassidy, "See, I bought a matching one for me."

The gift brought tears to my eyes. What a wonderful send off for my daughter leaving the security of elementary school for the big scary world of junior high. God bless our loving, kind teachers.

Cassidy at one year old.

Dylan, Summer (the tall ones), Channing and Cassidy

Channing and Cassidy at Easter

Cassidy (13) and Jadyn (9) 2013

GOD SENDS US A MESSAGE

My cousin, Cole, was marrying his true love, Jessica. We were so excited that they had decided to wed. Jessica and Cole were mature and had been in love for a long time and we were all ready to help them celebrate. Our family was excited about planning to attend the wedding in Austin the coming February.

Summer and Dylan, my sister's kids, were involved at their universities and with basketball, so they couldn't attend the wedding. Our daughter, Channing, was also involved in high school and classes she had signed up for.   Channing had never been very involved in athletics but had always been more interested in artistic endeavors. She was pouring all her time, energy, and money into creative lessons. Between her guitar, dance, singing, and acting lessons we seldom got to see

her. She had a part time job just to fund her artistic passions. We didn't have
to worry about her getting into trouble because she was too busy with school, homework, her part-time job, and various lessons to even squeeze us in at all!

It was February, 2012, and time for the big wedding. Everything was beautiful. The wedding and reception were at the same location in Austin. We arrived to see a large historical home with a huge, beautiful lawn filled with peacocks, casual seating and a place set up under the trees for the marriage vows. The weather cooperated with a sunny day and a cool temperature. The ceremony was sweet with a touch of humor. Afterward, we went inside for the reception and wandered around from table to table to find our place cards.

We found our assigned seats for dinner. Chad, Cassidy, and I were seated at a table with people we had never met before. I had always been an extrovert and most of my adult life had been in sales, so I enjoyed meeting new people. We all introduced ourselves and told how we were related to the bride and groom. I learned that the man sitting next to me was the bride's uncle, Kevin, from New Mexico. When dinner arrived, I took Cassidy's plate and cut her steak and passed it back to her. She was a mature twelve years old, which caused Kevin to look at me with a perplexed expression. I explained to him that she had a stroke either in utero or at birth, and that her entire right side did not fully function. He proceeded to tell me about a doctor in New Mexico that specialized in stroke victims in utero. I explained that we had taken Cassidy to Cooks Children's Hospital and Scottish Rite and countless therapists, and each of them had said that there was no cure. Kevin told me that the doctor used scalp acupuncture, and had amazing results with many neurologic diseases and disabilities. That was the craziest thing that I had ever heard. I knew about acupuncture and thought it was great for small ailments, aches and pains. My family was open to alternative therapies and not tied to allopathic medicine, but this sounded unbelievable. I probably would have just brushed off the information if it hadn't come from Jessica's uncle. I knew her family members were all highly educated professionals. They were very stable and credible people. He asked for my email address so he could send me more information on the acupuncturist in Santa Fe. I gave him one of my business cards and expected it to end there, never to hear from him again.

About a month after the wedding, I received an email from Kevin with information on Dr. Jason Hao. He also sent several links to articles written by him or about him. I forwarded the email to my mother. She and I began to research Dr. Hao and scalp acupuncture. Our research revealed that Dr. Hao had traveled to Walter Reed Hospital in Washington D.C. to teach and treat wounded veterans that had major trauma. Dr. Hao had great success with phantom limb pain and post- traumatic stress disorder. We saw videos that showed previously paralyzed veterans getting out of their wheelchairs and walking as a result of scalp acupuncture. All of the information was very impressive, but was so completely foreign to what I had been told was possible, that I brushed it off. Sometimes things sound just too good to be true. I had fallen for some of those during my life, and didn't want to feel like a fool again.

I had recently started a new job, and was stressed and busy trying to learn my new position. I didn't have any benefits, and knew I certainly couldn't ask for time off to take Cassidy to New Mexico for a long time. Mother and I still discussed different videos and articles we found, and shared information. After weeks of research and discussion, she called me and told me to book appointments for Cassidy. I protested telling her that I couldn't afford the trip, take off work from a new job, or pay for the treatments. I believed we should be able to find an acupuncturist in our highly populated Dallas – Fort Worth metroplex that could do scalp acupuncture. Mother suggested that I call Dr. Hao and ask for a referral to someone in our area that was qualified to do the scalp acupuncture that he performed. Before she hung up the phone, she said, "If there is no one closer to us, book the appointments. I will take both girls to New Mexico this summer. If it works, we will rejoice in a miracle. If it doesn't work, we will have a fun vacation together. Don't worry, your daddy and I will pay for the trip. If the treatments work even a little, it will be the best bargain I have ever received. There is no price on a miracle. If what we heard is true, these treatments could give Cassidy full use of her body. Besides, Cassidy deserves this chance. This could change her whole life, forever."

CHANGE IS A SCARY THING

Now it was time to break the news to Cassidy. One evening in May, I asked her to please sit with me on the couch. I explained to her that I was going to schedule an appointment for her to have a scalp acupuncture to help her right side.

Cassidy had a look of horror on her face. She started sobbing and shaking her head, "no". When she could catch her breath, she screamed at me, "I am happy the way I am! You can't make me, and if you do you will be the worst parent ever!"

Cassidy stood up, ready to flee the room. I held my hand up in the air, and sternly demanded her to sit down. We sat there quietly for a few minutes so we could calm down, and I could collect my thoughts.

I then agreed with her, "You are wonderful the way you are, but I would be a bad parent if I didn't make you try. I know other people who have had acupuncture done. They said it didn't hurt. There is no cutting, no healing time, and no medicine. It either works, or it doesn't. If it doesn't work, we would still have the same great Cassidy that we have now. Go to your room and make me a list of the pros and cons, and then we will discuss it when you're done."

Cassidy headed to her room still crying. I didn't see her again until bedtime when she came back into the den. I asked," Where is your list?"

"I will do it", she said pouting, "there are no cons."

I was so excited and proud of her. I gave her a big hug, and kissed her good night.

The next day, I called to book her appointment with Dr. Jason Hao. I learned that they suggested a series of treatments while we were in New Mexico. The price sounded very reasonable. I booked three appointments the second week in July.

My mother thought it would be fun for Channing to join Cassidy and her on the trip. Channing said she would be their photographer and videographer. We all wanted to go, but couldn't.

The pictures would help us to share in their adventures. Mother started preparing for the trip by booking hotel rooms and planning sightseeing adventures. She wanted them to have lots of great memories of their trip together, regardless of the success of Cassidy's treatments. Dr. Hao had offices in Albuquerque and Santa Fe. There was no way for them to do everything she had on her list of fun things to do and to see while there.

While helping Cassidy pack for the trip, I could tell that she was nervous about her upcoming treatments, and being away from home. I gave her a little pep talk, "Cassidy, I know that God has great things planned for you. You have to believe it, too."

The following day Channing, Cassidy, and mother began their ten hour drive to New Mexico.

They planned to drive halfway, and spend their first night in Amarillo. I had the worst knots in my stomach. I was sad and filled with regret that Chad and I weren't able to take her. I knew they were in good hands. Channing promised to keep us updated by phone, and to video the high points of their trip. We were especially happy that she was going to video her treatments.

The girls called the first night when they checked into their hotel room in Amarillo, Texas. They told me that they were about to go eat dinner, and that Mom Mom fell and hurt her foot walking into the motel. Before I went to bed that night, I called to check on Mother. She told me that her right foot was swollen and turning black and blue. She made light of her injury by saying, "I will be just fine."

Early the next morning they headed to Santa Fe, New Mexico. Once they arrived Mother went to buy Epsom Salts to soak her foot. It had continued to swell and become more painful. When I spoke to Cassidy, she seemed to be in a bad mood. She was homesick and nervous about her first treatment the next day. I felt terrible that I wasn't there with her. I wanted to be there to give her a big hug, and assure her that everything was going to be okay. I went to bed that night and prayed for my mother's foot to feel better. I also prayed for God to use Dr. Hao to help Cassidy to be helped in a mighty way.

MY CUP RUNNETH OVER

I woke the next morning filled with anxiety and "what ifs". What if the scalp acupuncture doesn't work? What if it is painful? What if she needs me? I kept looking at the clock to see if it was time for her appointment. My eyes kept welling up with tears. Just before it was time for her appointment, I received a text message from Channing. It was a picture of Cassidy standing outside the doctor's office. The text read, "About to walk in with butterflies."

I replied, "I can see them. Tell her the butterflies are her angels looking over her."

When it was time for lunch, I went home to await her call. About an hour later, I received the call. I heard Cassidy say, "Mom, guess what? I was able to pick up a pen, and a cell phone. I opened the car door! I did it all with my right hand!"

I began to weep with tears of joy. Cassidy asked, "Mom, are you crying?"

Between sobs, I said, "Yes, I am just so very happy for you. Did it hurt?"

Cassidy said, "No, not at all. Guess what! I have all my vision! I can see my hair on the right side of my face! I will call you later. We are about to order lunch."

After we hung up, I rushed to tell Chad the good news. We both agreed that this was the most amazing thing ever. How in the world could putting needles in someone's head or body make them suddenly be able to regain eyesight? How could these needles help her to use her right hand that had always been in a fist? Chad seemed skeptical. He said, "I have to see it to believe it." I kept thinking, "Why?" Why hadn't we heard about this before? We had met so many children like Cassidy over the last 12 years. Why didn't any of us ever hear about scalp acupuncture? I knew they would all want this chance for improvement.

Late in the afternoon, my mother called. She was going to the store for more medicine for her foot. She had left the girls at the hotel, and wanted to share more of what happened at the doctor's office. She told me how emotionally drained she was. She had also been filled with anticipation and trepidation. We had all been wound up tight not knowing what the outcome would be. Mother said, "Allison, as soon as Dr. Hao started putting needles in Cassidy's head, she started crying. Cassidy exclaimed that she had feeling and sensation on her right side for the first time in her life. It was overwhelming. It was worth the trip just for her to get feeling on her right side! Dr. Hao even videotaped Cassidy doing a series of exercises. He had her to open and close both hands, point and flex her toes, and walk up and down the hall. He wants to keep a record of her progress. He even asked Channing to video tape the whole appointment.

He wants her to show it to the family, and anyone who wants to see how this works.

He would place the needles and let her just sit for five to ten minutes. Then he would ask her to do the exercises again. He would then spin some needles, and place new needles in other places. He repeated this over and over. Each time he would check her, the results were better. I have laughed and cried all afternoon. I feel that someone has just pulled my emotional plug. It has been overwhelming in a wonderful way.

That evening I received a phone call from Cassidy. I couldn't understand a word she was saying due to a bad case of the giggles. Mother took the phone away and said that Cassidy had giggled that way ever since they had left the doctor's office. They didn't have an appointment the next day because the offices were closed. She and the girls had decided to spend the day sightseeing. They spent the morning around the square in Santa Fe. There were vendors selling handmade jewelry and crafts around the square, lots of interesting shops, and wonderful restaurants. The day lasted as long as she could hobble around on her injured foot. She had been having trouble with sciatica in her left hip when she left home. Now with her right foot swollen and in pain, she didn't know how long she could hold out. Mother was very determined that this would still be a fun trip that none of them would ever forget. Family bonding time, good food, interesting sights, history, art, and miracles were on her agenda.

Nothing was going to change her mind unless the pain screamed for her to stop. One thing was for sure; they would never be able to forget this miracle trip!

Next, they went to the famous Chapel of Our Lady of Light, also known as Loretto Chapel. The story behind Loretto is the story of a miracle. How appropriate for this trip! Their next adventure was to go to Chimayo. They enjoyed the drive there through the red mountains and hills. There was a tiny chapel there where many testify to having had miraculous healings. There is a room next door to the chapel where people have left their wheelchairs and crutches to prove their healing. Cassidy was seeing yet another testament to the possibilities of miracles. Thursday morning they drove an hour to Albuquerque for their next appointment. Dr. Hao and his wife Linda are both from China, and learned scalp acupuncture at a university there. Mother was overwhelmed at their kind, caring treatment of our whole family. Dr. Hao had been so complimentary of Channing. He knew from experience how hard she had worked to be a help to Cassidy. He understood how much work and time it took to assist a person that had physical limitations. Mother and Channing loved the joy he showed when Cassidy showed improvement in any of her exercises. He praised her efforts, and explained to her how hard she would have to work to make muscles and nerves work that had never been able to before. He would tell her that he did his part to reconnect the signals, now it was up to her to build them up. When I talked to Mother on the phone, she would constantly tell me how Dr. Hao had an aura of love and joy. Mother said she was just as excited to see him as Cassidy was.

Mother and the girls even loved the artwork in their offices. They learned that Dr. Jason Hao had painted them, and showed them in the local art galleries. Mother had already decided to buy one for Cassidy as a forever memento of her healing trip to New Mexico. Cassidy wanted to put it at the end of her bed. She could be reminded every morning when she opened her eyes that she had received a miracle.

Cassidy's second treatment helped in small degrees of movement in her hand, wrist, and ankle. It didn't seem like much compared to her first treatment. Dr. Hao kept reminding her to keep exercising these joints and force herself to use her right side. Almost thirteen years of habits are hard to break. Before they left his office, he asked if they could come back to Albuquerque on Saturday. He normally never opened on Saturday, but he was going to see a three year old flying in from North Carolina on Saturday. He said that as long as he was going to be at the office he would love to give Cassidy a fourth treatment. Mother took this as another blessing. The trip from Arlington, Texas was long and tiring, so any extra treatments were a bonus.

On the way back to Santa Fe, Channing, Cassidy, and mother took the Turquoise Trail. The alternate route gave them more opportunities to enjoy the beautiful vistas of desert and mountains. Small shops along the way supplied lots of opportunities to see local arts and crafts. They found more tempting handmade local jewelry to add to their stash to take home.

Each treatment continued to show positive results. Throughout the week Channing continued to text me
pictures with needles in various parts of Cassidy's body. Each day she would have a needle in her ear and anywhere from two to five in her head, usually around the crown of her scalp. Sometimes needles would be in her head, hand, elbow, knee, ankle, or

foot. She left Friday's treatment, in Santa Fe, happy with an original painting done by Dr. Jason Hao. She loved the painting, but she really loved the artist even more.

Saturday was the last treatment for the trip. When they arrived, they met the couple from North Carolina, and their three year old son. He had also been born with a stroke in utero. His stroke had affected his speech. Dr. Hao was busy going from room to room seeing both of his patients. He allowed mother and the girls to view videos of several of his previous patients while they were waiting for Cassidy's turn. The patients in the videos ranged in age from three to eighty. They had come to get treatments for strokes, Parkinson's, Multiple Sclerosis, seizures, and phantom limb pain. They were telling about their symptoms and disabilities then showing their improvements. Before they left his office, Dr. Hao told Cassidy that he wanted her to return for more treatments before school started. He also told her that he wanted to see her tie her own shoes using both hands when she returned in August.

HOME AGAIN, HOME AGAIN, JIGGITY JIG

Mom called us from Amarillo, and told us when they should be arriving home. Chad and I went to my parent's house to greet them a little early. Chad and I definitely wanted to be there when they arrived home. We wanted to see the changes in Cassidy with our own eyes. We took roses for Mom and balloons for Cassidy. We were on pins and needles waiting impatiently for them to arrive. Within the hour, we saw the car pulling into the driveway. It seemed to take forever for them to get out of the car. I watched Cassidy get out of the car and stretch. She reached her arms out in front of her, interlaced her fingers and raised her arms above her head. My mouth dropped open. I looked at Dad and Chad and said, "Did you just see that? That is unbelievable! There is no way she could have done that before the treatments!"

Dad, Chad, and I rushed out to help unload the bags and suitcases. When we were all in the game room, I handed Cassidy her balloons. Then we all took turns giving hugs. I was stunned. Cassidy hugged me back. She used both arms and hands for the first time in her life. She couldn't wait to show us all the different things she could do with her right hand. She opened a door, picked up a bag, a book, and a pen with her right hand. Then she said, "Oh, yeah, shake my hand. See, I have a grip now."

That ability really thrilled her. She had always been embarrassed to shake hands. When she worked to open her right hand, her fingers would go in all directions. She had no control over them. Then her hand and fingers would be sweaty from being fisted. She felt that it was calling attention to her impairments. Most people were kind and understanding about it, but it was humiliating for her.

A few days after their return, Mother went to an orthopedic doctor and learned that she had broken three metatarsal bones in her right foot. None of the family could believe that she was able to tolerate all the sightseeing, driving, and constant activity they crammed into their trip.

Mother saw it as a God thing. She said that ice, Epsom salts, ibuprofen, and naproxen sodium got her through the pain. She said that since she had to put all her weight on her left foot, she realized that is what Cassidy had been forced to do her whole life. She became aware of how exhausting it was to walk, and to be concerned over every step she took.

My mother couldn't stop talking about how she had felt God's hand in every aspect of their trip. The Hotel had offered reduced rates and worked to get her a room on the first floor close to the front door. She even felt it was part of God's plan that she broke her foot during the trip. Dr. Hao had impressed her as the most caring, loving doctor that she had ever met. Of course, the biggest sign to her was the miraculous improvements that Cassidy had over the course of one week. Our prayers for Cassidy were being answered in dramatic fashion.

Dr. Hao called about a week after Cassidy returned home to check on her progress, and to recommend physical therapy. I asked him if she would need acupuncture for the rest of her life. He replied, "I would like to see her again before school starts in the fall. She needs a few more treatments. That is it. She is healed. It will take time for her hand, foot, arm, and leg muscles to grow and develop, of course. We just need to give her body time to catch up."

Cassidy and Matthew with Dr. Hao.

Cassidy with needles in her scalp.

SPREADING THE GOOD NEWS

The good news about Cassidy's successful treatments was spreading. Each family member was sharing the good news through phone calls, social media, at work, at church, and by telling anyone else who would listen. We all wanted to share her story, because we felt it offered so many people hope for improvement and healing in their lives. We knew that healing someone also helped their whole family.   We felt it was imperative to spread the great news.

Tracy was a friend of my sister, Alicia. Tracy's son, Matthew, had also been born with a stroke in utero. He was a year older than Cassidy, and his condition was almost the same as hers. His impairments were also on his right side.   For the last five years, Tracy, Matthew, Cassidy and I had done things together occasionally. We thought our kids would be able to relate to each other, and enjoy the freedom of not worrying with the feeling of being judged.

I called Tracy, and we set up a meeting for lunch to "show and tell' them about Dr. Hao. I brought a book that my mother had purchased online. The book, <u>Chinese Scalp Acupuncture</u>, was written by Dr. Jason Hao, and his wife, Dr. Linda Hao. The book was written primarily to train and educate acupuncturists. It explains how to do it, case studies, and lists of conditions that can be helped or cured by scalp acupuncture. I wanted to tell Cassidy's story, and the book would help me fill in facts. After hearing the information and seeing Cassidy, they agreed to go to New Mexico. It was the middle of July, and we were all planning a trip for the middle of August. Tracy and I were able to book appointments with Dr. Hao the second week in August. We hoped Cassidy would help give Matthew courage and support.

The first week of August was the time for Cassidy's annual checkup for both orthopedic and neurology at Scottish Rite Hospital. I couldn't wait for them to see the dramatic changes in Cassidy's mobility, and her improvements. Mother had been busy for the last two weeks doing more research on Chinese scalp acupuncture. She had put together a large stack of articles on Dr. Hao and Chinese scalp acupuncture, and put them into folders. I was so excited to take Cassidy to Scottish Rite armed with informational folders, and Dr. Hao's book to show her doctors.

Her first appointment was with the orthopedic doctor. When he entered the room, he was accompanied by several other physicians. I told them about the acupuncture treatments, and handed them one of the packets. The orthopedic doctor watched her walk and nodded his head. He said, "Very good. Have you seen the neurologist yet?" He quickly wrapped things up and sent us to the neurology department.

When we were in the neurologist's office, the nurse came into the room. I guess the other doctors from orthopedics had already sent word about our story. She immediately said, "I hear that some things have changed since your last visit." I filled her in on Cassidy's treatments, showed her the packet, and Dr. Hao's book. She asked to look at them. I handed them to her, and exclaimed how successful the treatments had been. She took them as she left the room, and said, "We'll see about that. I'll go get the doctor." I felt she was dismissing my information and Cassidy's improvements. At first, I was annoyed by the reaction that I was receiving. Then I remembered how ridiculous it had sounded when I first heard about scalp acupuncture a few months earlier. Her reaction was typical. It did seem too unbelievable.

The neurologist finally entered the room followed by several other doctors and nurses. He sat down and said, "I understand some things have changed for you because of acupuncture."

I corrected him by adding, "scalp acupuncture". That was my last chance to say anything for a while.

Cassidy spoke up for herself and told them her story, which really shocked me. She had always been quiet and shy. Instead of telling her order to a waiter or waitress at a restaurant, she would have one of us order for her. She felt especially intimidated speaking to adults. Our old Cassidy would have never spoken to a group of professional adults for any reason. Now, our new Cassidy wanted to tell her own story. Who was this child? I was speechless as she told the room full of doctors and nurses about the acupuncture treatments, the instant improvement in sight, gaining physical sensations, and what all she could do now with her right side. One benefit that I was just seeing was a new found confidence and self-assurance. These doctors couldn't measure that, but it was a huge benefit that I was seeing for the first time.

We continued to get raised eyebrows and apprehensive looks. The neurologist had her to do some exercises with her right hand. Then he got a device that measures muscle tone. He had used this device before putting her on Artane. Back then, when he placed the devise on her impaired right side I would hear a loud static noise. When it was placed on her good left side, it was silent. Now when he placed it on her right arm and leg there was no static. The only place that the machine made static was on her right hand. The doctor turned and looked at me and said, "Mom, I'm equally impressed. I want you to schedule another Assisting Hand Assessment test. I want them to measure her new results. "

When I took her back for the AHA test, the therapist offered to work with Cassidy on her therapy. I scheduled several appointments that wouldn't interfere with school. When we returned for her

next therapy session the therapist asked detailed questions about the scalp acupuncture. We discussed everything that I could think to tell her. Then she said, "Mrs. Moore, Cassidy's scores came back with substantial results. Her score went up 12 points to a 54. The angle of her right arm went from a 25 degree angle to a 20 degree angle. These results
are remarkable. Her neurologist wants to learn more about Dr. Hao."

I gave her another one of Dr. Hao's business cards. I told her what Dr. Hao had said to me, "You tell Scottish Rite that I come teach them. I want to help children. We need more doctors to do this. Many children need help."

A few days later, Cassidy, Channing, and I headed off to New Mexico for her second set of treatments. These trips were expensive so we all tried to save money every way we could. We drove straight through the night with Channing and I taking turns behind the wheel. She was thrilled to drive, and I loved having some relief every few hours. We met up with Tracy and Matthew in Santa Fe. They had flown in for his first set of treatments. She worked as a flight attendant so they could save by flying.

We shared my car which helped with not having to rent one. When we arrived early the next morning, they let us borrow their room for a few hours so we could get a nap. The 10 hour drive had worn us out. We definitely wanted to be rested and ready for Cassidy and Matthew's afternoon appointments. That afternoon the kids' appointments were 30 minutes apart. Dr. Hao was kind to let their appointments be one after the other. Matthew was first, and he was terrified. Dr. Hao started with Cassidy. He put needles in her head to demonstrate that it didn't hurt. If a girl could do it, we knew Matthew would want to prove that he could too.

Both Cassidy and Matthew showed improvement that week in their control and use of their right hand and walking straighter. They tended to throw their bad leg out to the side, because their joints had been locked up. Matthew's improvements were not as dramatic as Cassidy's first treatments had been, but every person reacts differently. Dr. Hao told us that some have immediate success, while others may take 10 or 15 or 20 treatments.

When Dr. Hao was finished with their treatments on the last day, he put them in different rooms. He tore off large sheets of paper that he used to cover the patient tables where patients lie down for treatments. Each of the kids was given a sheet of paper and told to write a sentence using their right hand that had been useless. Dr. Hao said," I want you to write something about acupuncture."

The kids went to separate rooms. When they came out, we all laughed. They had both written,

 "Acupuncture has changed my life!" We couldn't believe they had both written exactly the same sentence. Laughter and tears were all a part of these trips and appointments. Years of worry and stress, joy, and relief all bubbled to the surface.

While we were at Dr. Hao's office that week, he asked us if we wanted to come watch one of his patients who had a virus attack his spinal cord. The virus left his legs paralyzed, and he was going to try and walk for the first time after treatment. In fact, it had been five years since he had walked. We watched him get up and walk, with assistance, down the hall.

Another day, when we arrived, Dr. Hao said that he had a great morning. He had been called to help a boy who was in a coma. Other doctors had given up on him and didn't think he would ever wake from his coma. Dr. Hao said, "It was good! He woke up! It was a great day!"

Cassidy was now able to walk on her tippy toes for a short distance and balance on her right leg. Throwing and catching a small ball became a fun learning activity. She even practiced writing with her right hand in a journal on the trip home. It seemed she was gaining agility, balance, movement, and confidence with every treatment.

GAINING GROUND

Just like most children, Cassidy had never looked forward to the new school year starting. New teachers, new students, and new situations made her especially nervous. Classwork had always been a struggle for her, so that added more anxiety. Cassidy's first year in junior high school was about to start in a few weeks, and for the first time she was excited. That really shocked the whole family, because a few months earlier she had been filled with dread and trepidation. Her new gained confidence had filled her with new plans and ideas.

Her first plan was to get in touch with her special needs teacher in elementary school. Cassidy couldn't wait to show her the physical progress she had made. She also wanted to get in touch with a younger student, Cayden, who was in third grade.

He had the same condition as she had, but he was affected even more. The teacher agreed to pass on the information about Dr. Hao to his family. Cayden's mother contacted me within a few days. When she heard the story, she booked appointments with Dr. Hao. I quickly booked appointments in October, the same dates as the Cayden's appointments.

My aunt and uncle, Virginia and Dale, love to travel and love Cassidy. They volunteered to take her for her next appointments in October. They made arrangements to be at Dr. Hao's office for Cayden's first appointment. Cayden was terrified of the needles, and began to scream and cry. Dr. Hao went to the waiting room and asked Cassidy to please come into the treatment room with Cayden. Dr. Hao asked if he could put a needle into her head to show Cayden that it didn't hurt. Cassidy happily agreed and said, "See, it doesn't hurt at all."

Dr. Hao told Cayden's family that if Cassidy hadn't been there he wouldn't have been able to treat him. During his second treatment the following day, Cayden told Dr. Hao, "You program the needles to tell my legs what do. "

Dr. Hao replied, "Yes, I guess you're right."

A few days after the October treatments, I received a text message from Cassidy's former teacher. She stated, "Cayden was big man on campus today. He was so excited he was coming out of his skin. He was showing everyone how he could control his thumb, and lay his hand flat on his paper when writing. He showed how strong his impaired hand was if he used his brain. He was walking better and able to cross his impaired leg over the other one. Very impressive! Thanks again to Cassidy for helping. Hopefully, he will go again for more sessions."

I didn't notice any new physical changes in Cassidy, but her self-confidence continued to grow at school. In the past, she could learn and understand math during class, but would not remember how to do it for homework. We would help her at home on how to do the problems, but the next day she would have to start all over again. Chad and I had always had to help her for hours every night to keep up with her homework. It was tiring and frustrating for Cassidy and for us. We were totally shocked when after Christmas break, she informed us that she no longer needed our help with homework. "Now I can see the problems in my head, so I can figure them out. Before my

140

treatments, I could never visualize the numbers in my head," she said with a huge smile on her face. School was still a challenge because she had so much catching up to do, but she knew she could do it.

 Cassidy had always loved helping other children with special needs at school and at church. Now it was a passion for her. Because of her life experiences, she had an abundance of patience and understanding for others with   disabilities or challenges. Where she had always been afraid and timid, she now wanted to speak for herself and tell her story. We were witnessing her metamorphosis. She was breaking free of her cocoon and beginning to spread her wings. Her greatest desire became a passion to help spread the word of healing and hope for others.

Ever since Cassidy's first treatment, her right side had continued to change. Her right side had always been smaller than her left.   It was now growing and catching up with her left side. She was overjoyed when she realized one day that she could actually see the bones in her right hand and foot. She had never been able to see them before. Her right hand had always been like a limp rag with no strength or pressure.   Muscles, nerves, and tendons were all beginning to grow and become more functional. When we told people after her first trip to New Mexico of her successful treatments, they expected her to look totally different. What they didn't understand was that it would take time for her right side to catch up with her left. The trips to New Mexico took time and money, but we felt that this was the best money we had ever spent. Some of her problems were totally cured, others were improving slowly but surely. That was huge! No one had ever given us any hope for improving at all. Her past physical therapies had only helped to train her on how to deal with her disabilities. From now on, we knew she would be able to tackle her own hygiene, chores, and schoolwork. In the future, we now felt she could look forward to becoming a wife and mother and all that entailed. We had always told her that she could be whatever she wanted to be, but we worried about how difficult that could be for her. Now we knew her chances at a happy, healthy life had increased dramatically. We thanked God and Dr. Hao for the blessings we had been given.

I DON'T JUST BELIEVE, I KNOW!

Proverbs 3:5

Trust in the Lord with all your heart and lean not on your own understanding.

There are so many things that are beyond my understanding. How is it possible that God loves and seeks a relationship with every person in the world? That doesn't make any sense to me. I have met a lot of crazy, scary people that I have no desire to have a relationship with. I don't understand why or how Cassidy and I survived her birth. Nor do I understand the angels carrying away my pain and immediately after that, my liver and kidneys began to function. I have been told several times in the

143

last 13 years that it is very rare for a pregnant woman to survive HELLP in eclampsia. I don't understand how acupuncture works. With only a few acupuncturists in the world that do scalp acupuncture, how were we in the right place at the right time to learn about Dr. Hao?

I do know that God cares and is very precise with who he puts in your life. Sitting next to Kevin Hennelly at my cousins wedding reception changed our lives. I also learned that the phrase,

 "God doesn't call the equipped, he equips the called" is true. I feel that God told me to write this book and share Cassidy's story to help His other children. I was excited to tell her story, but sitting still to write a book was a daunting task. I don't even like to write for emails, tweets, or Facebook. I informed God that he had chosen the wrong person to write a book. At the time, I was unemployed and needed to find a job to help support our family. Phone calls kept coming from friends and strangers that were hearing of Cassidy's story. With every phone call or email, I could hear God telling me that he was going to see to it that I remained unemployed until I wrote the book. It became very clear to me that I was his servant. He didn't bless us with Cassidy's healing for us to keep it for ourselves. He blessed us so we would bless others. He truly loves and cares for those who are suffering and wants each of us to know there is hope. I just had to keep reaffirming, "I can do all things through Christ who strengthens me."

USING YOUR HEAD

Most people have heard of acupuncture. Many have used it to fix problems such as headaches, body aches, pain, and weight loss, even to quit smoking. Although we have heard success stories from friends and family, we don't try it. Allopathic medicine is what we are familiar with because alternative therapies are not as well known or accepted in western culture. We often tend to feel safer with traditional medicine because it is what we know something about. Many people have insurance policies that don't cover acupuncture, and that causes them to not try it. Many insurance companies have been slow to accept any alternative therapies, even after they have been proven to work. Sometimes we try a different method because we don't like the side effects of prescription drugs. People often don't use an alternative method of healing unless they feel traditional medicine hasn't helped them. It becomes a last resort.

If a person has been given no hope for improvement, and is suffering from loss of function, mobility, or any of their senses, wouldn't they love being made whole? Wouldn't they love just regaining any of their lost abilities? When we heard of scalp acupuncture, we felt we had nothing to lose. If Cassidy regained any of her disabilities of feeling, sight, movement, balance, use of limbs, use of hand or foot, it was worth a try. At least with scalp acupuncture, there was the possibility of some or all being given to her. The only other options that had been mentioned to us over the years were the use of Botox and umbilical cord therapy. Botox was said to offer the possibility of relaxing the muscles in Cassidy's right hand and arm. It was experimental at that time, and she would have multiple shots every 3 to 4 months. The doctors felt that the Botox could give her use of her hand and arm if she received treatments the rest of her life. That would be very expensive with unknown results.

The umbilical cord therapy was a huge problem. We had not saved her umbilical cord when she was born. There were too many emergencies going on at the time of her birth for us to think of that. We were going to have to use the umbilical cord of her cousin, Jadyn. The chance of a compatible match was very slim. The cord therapy would have been thousands of dollars with only a slim chance of a compatible match, and no confidence that it would work. It was still in the experimental stages at that time.

The possibility that there was a therapy available that could actually heal some or all of her problems had never been suggested to us in her 13 years. We would have been thrilled if she had any improvement with scalp acupuncture. We never dreamed that she would continue to improve with each series of treatments. Who would have ever guessed that her schoolwork would become much easier? That alone would have been worth the treatments.

Each person and condition reacts differently with scalp acupuncture. Acupuncture may take three or four treatments, or it might take up to 20. That is usually true of any kind of medical treatment for major injury or illness. Cassidy always wanted to go back for more treatments, because she always gained from every one of them. The family often didn't see much progress after some of her treatments, but she felt they were working. We couldn't know how much she was gaining from unseen problems. We had to trust that she knew her own body. All we knew is that Cassidy was doing things she never had been able to do, and she was happier than she had ever been.

Acupuncture has been used for three thousand years in the east, but is relatively new to the west. Scalp acupuncture originated approximately 40 years ago in China. It enables people to be helped who previously were thought to be beyond help. It has been especially helpful for those with neurological problems and those with spinal cord injuries. Acupuncturists and western allopathic doctors are using it to help patients who were previously thought to be beyond help.

According to Dr. Hao, "scalp acupuncture not only treats disorders, but can also prevent illness and help to build the immune system. It can increase energy, preserve youth, and promote longevity". It does not require drugs or surgery.   It is affordable especially compared to other clinical options. It cost less than most insurance deductibles. We have been telling Cassidy's story to numerous people with illnesses and disabilities that scalp acupuncture could help them or their family member. Many people find it difficult to believe it could help them. I assume people relate it to a "get rich quick" scheme. It seems too good to be true. When doctors, nurses, and therapists continually tell you that there is little that can be done, you lose hope. It hurts to have your hopes built up for a cure, or even an improvement, and then discover it offers nothing. It also cost so much to try all the different therapies, machines, medicines, and appointments that offer the possibility of improvement. Patients and their families feel drained emotionally, physically, and financially. Some people are even afraid that it would make their condition worse. The unknown can be terrifying, especially when you are already suffering. There are a few people with disabilities that feel that they know how to deal with their current health problems, but aren't sure how they could adjust to any changes.

Our first reaction upon hearing the possibility of healing through scalp acupuncture was, "Why haven't we ever heard anything about this before?

If it can really heal people, wouldn't it be all over the news?"

This is one of the first questions that everyone asks upon hearing of Cassidy's healing. In the Haos' book, Chinese Scalp Acupuncture, they list the 4 main reasons it is not more widely used. "First, up to now there has been no authoritative and practical text for scalp acupuncture in English. Second, there are a very limited number of highly experienced teachers. Third, manual manipulation is very difficult to learn and master without detailed description and demonstration. And fourth, the names of stimulation areas are different from the standardized names given by the Standard International Acupuncture Nomenclature of the World Health Organization, Section 3.6 on Scalp Acupuncture, in Geneva in 1989."

The Haos' also state "that there have been few reports or articles published on treatment by scalp acupuncture. Most existing textbooks either lack detailed information or only introduce some new research on the topic. From their teachers and textbooks, students can learn only general information about scalp acupuncture and its locations and clinical applications.

Therefore, many practitioners in both the West and the East are only mildly aware of this new technique, and few apply it in their practices. There is a high demand for a book that can provide teachers and students with useful knowledge and offer proper references to experienced practitioners. We feel confident that this book (Chinese Scalp Acupuncture) will meet these requirements."

What is so wonderful about scalp acupuncture is that it seldom hurts at all. If there is discomfort, the patient just tells the doctor and the needle is readjusted.   The more relaxed and calm the patient is seems to aid the acupuncture's success. The doctor places needles where they are needed for the patient's condition. Then the patient just sits or lies calmly and waits for the doctor to adjust or spin the needles. The experience can be very soothing and calming. In some cases, it causes bouts of laughter and giggles when the patient gets immediate relief from pain, or new sensation of feeling in numb limbs, or new sight in eyes fogged from stroke, or can speak words that have been wanting to be said, but couldn't be.

Some conditions can get immediate relief within only a few treatments. For those that have suffered for years with a malady, it could take a series of treatments that cover months. We took Cassidy for a week of treatments in the months of July, August, October, and March for a total of 17. For our daughter, Cassidy, it has taken a year to get all the success we wanted. That was because she had never been able to use her right hand or arm since birth. The arm had not grown normally because of not being used. It took time for it to grow and become strong enough to function as she wanted it to. Now she can even see her bones and veins in her hand and foot for the first time. It isn't magic. The patient has to do therapy on their own to help their body to readjust to new found abilities. It also takes persistence in relearning how to maneuver in the world.

Cassidy found it difficult to reach out and do things with a hand she had never been able to use. Old habits die hard.

It has amazed us how many people are afraid to try Chinese scalp acupuncture, yet will let a doctor try experimental surgery or take powerful, expensive drugs with possible serious side-effects in hopes of alleviating some of their symptoms. Does everyone that receives treatments become 100% better? No, but everyone we know, or have heard stories about, has been vastly improved. When an elderly patient has been wheel chair bound for years, they are happy to be able to walk with a cane. When you haven't been able to ever participate in any sports because of brain trauma, and then you can throw and catch a ball, swim, and try new tasks, it is empowering. Nothing is more empowering than to be able to take care of one's own needs.

With most brain traumas and diseases, the patient is usually told things will never change. If anything, they are told they will probably decline over time. We felt that it was worth the time, money and effort to give Cassidy the opportunity for a normal life, with full use of her whole body. It was the best money we ever spent. We knew that miracles were still happening. We saw it with our own eyes. Cassidy was overjoyed after her first appointment.

Dr. Jason Hao, and his wife Dr. Linda Hao, are well trained in scalp acupuncture. They trained with the leaders in the field of scalp acupuncture while they were at Heilongjiang University in China. The doctors have been teaching, practicing, and researching acupuncture for 31 years.

The doctors have been practicing in the United States for over 24 years. Doctors Jason and Linda Hao have a joint practice in Santa Fe and Albuquerque, New Mexico. They also spend as much time as possible training other acupuncturists in the use of these techniques locally and around the world.

Dr. Jason Hao is the president of the International Academy of Scalp Acupuncture. He is the chairman of the Acupuncture Committee at the National Certification Commission for Acupuncture and Oriental Medicine (NCCAOM). He is the vice-president of the Southwest Acupuncture College Board in Santa Fe, New Mexico. Dr. Jason Hao has had case studies published in the U.S. Army publication Stripes, in China Daily, Alternative Therapies, and Global Advances.

Dr. Jason Hao has trained many doctors, and treated thousands of patients in the United States and Europe. In the last 11 years, he has held seminars sponsored by Stanford, UCLA, and a seminar at Walter Reed Medical Center in Washington D.C.

Dr. Linda Hao has been published in Acupuncture Today, Chinese Journal of Information of Traditional Chinese Medicine, and The World Federation of Acupuncture in Beijing. She specializes in fibromyalgia and traumatic brain injury.

We need more acupuncturists trained in scalp acupuncture. It isn't economically feasible for some people to travel to New Mexico several times in a year for treatments. Certainly, all acupuncturists don't want to practice scalp acupuncture. They are happy with what they are doing and their level of expertise. There are also many that want to learn all new techniques that could help more people. We discovered that some acupuncturists also practiced chiropractic medicine. These methods work very well together. Doctors of acupuncture don't make large sums of money in the United States because the majority of the public either is unfamiliar with it, or their insurance doesn't cover it in their state. More doctors need to be informed about scalp acupuncture, and we need to have a fund available to help them to finance their training. An additional problem is that there are few highly experienced teachers in the field in the United States.

There are many clinical applications for scalp acupuncture. In Dr. Jason Hao, and Dr. Linda Hao's book, <u>Chinese Scalp Acupuncture</u>, the applications listed are:

Paralysis

Stroke

Dysphagia

Multiple Sclerosis

Spinal cord injury

Traumatic Brain Injury

Monoplegia (Hemiplegia)

Bell's Palsy

Motor Neuron Disease

Pain

Phantom Limb Pain

Complex Regional Pain

Residual Limb Pain

Plantar Fasciitis

Restless Leg Syndrome

Fibromyalgia

Herpes Zoster

Low Back Pain

Aphasia

Expressive Aphasia

Receptive Aphasia

Anomic Aphasia

Spasmodic Dysphonia

Vocal Cord Paralysis

Sense Organ Disorders

Meniere's Disease

Tinnitus

Hearing Loss

Vision Loss

Diplopia (Double Vision)

Female and Male Disorders

Uterine Bleeding

Impotence or Erectile Dysfunction

Male Infertility

Pediatric Disorders

Attention Deficit Disorder

Down's Syndrome

Seizure

Pediatric Aphasia

Additional Neuropsychological Disorders

Post-traumatic Stress disorder

Post-concussion Syndrome

Parkinson's Disease

Chorea

Ataxia

Alzheimer's Disease

Essential Tremor

Coma

Chronic Fatigue Syndrome

Descriptions of case studies are in their book, Chinese Scalp Acupuncture. This book was written for doctors wanting to learn the techniques, but is full of great information on how these were treated and success stories. We were able to purchase our copy of the book through Amazon.

A LETTER FROM CASSIDY

I wouldn't change what has happened to me. Without being who I am, I wouldn't be able to have the opportunities to inspire and help others. If my story can help even one person to get treated and have hope, then it is all worth it. I was happy with who and how I was before having scalp acupuncture, but it has truly changed my life!

To all the people out there that have a disability and feel worthless, get bullied or feel hopeless; I want you to know there is hope!

Yours truly,
Cassidy Moore (13)

505-986-0542
Dr Jason Hao
Santa Fe NM
drmihaly-acupuncture.com
drmihaly-acupuncture.com
scalpacumaster.com

Dr Hongzhen Chen
HZ Acupuncture
972-401-1818
7423 Las Colinas Blvd
Suite 103
Irving TX

162